FOR ORGANS, PIANOS & ELECTRONIC KEYBOARDS

E-Z PLAY® TODAY

323

MW00826811

HIGH SCHOOL MUSICAL

ISBN 978-1-4234-5116-7

Disney characters and artwork © Disney Enterprises, Inc.

Walt Disney Music Company
Wonderland Music Company, Inc.

DISTRIBUTED BY

7777 W. BLUEMOUND RD. P.O. BOX 13819 MILWAUKEE, WI 53213

In Australia Contact:
Hal Leonard Australia Pty. Ltd.
4 Lentara Court
Cheltenham, Victoria, 3192 Australia
Email: ausadmin@halleonard.com

Visit Hal Leonard Online at
www.halleonard.com

Start of Something New

Registration 4
Rhythm: 8 Beat or Rock

Words and Music by Matthew Gerrard
and Robbie Nevil

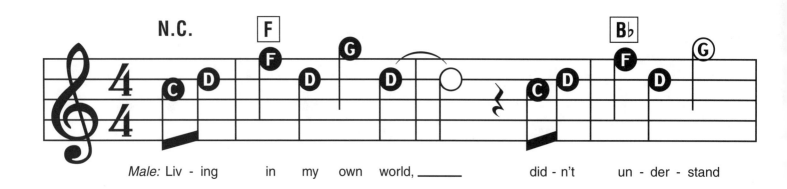

Male: Liv - ing in my own world, _____ did - n't un - der - stand

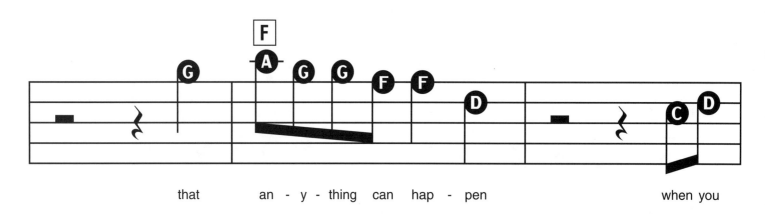

that an - y - thing can hap - pen when you

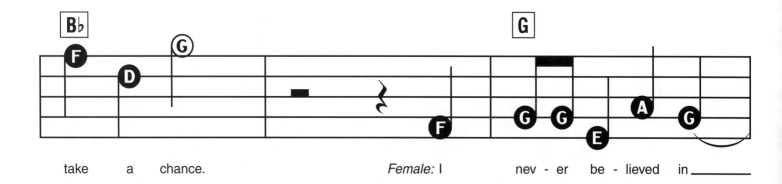

take a chance. Female: I nev - er be - lieved in _____

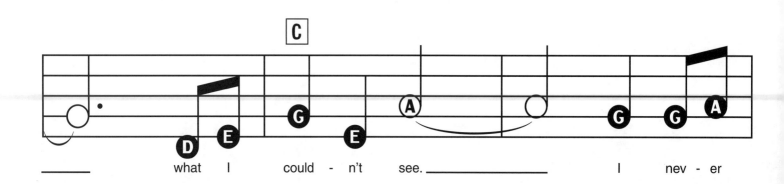

_____ what I could - n't see. _____ I nev - er

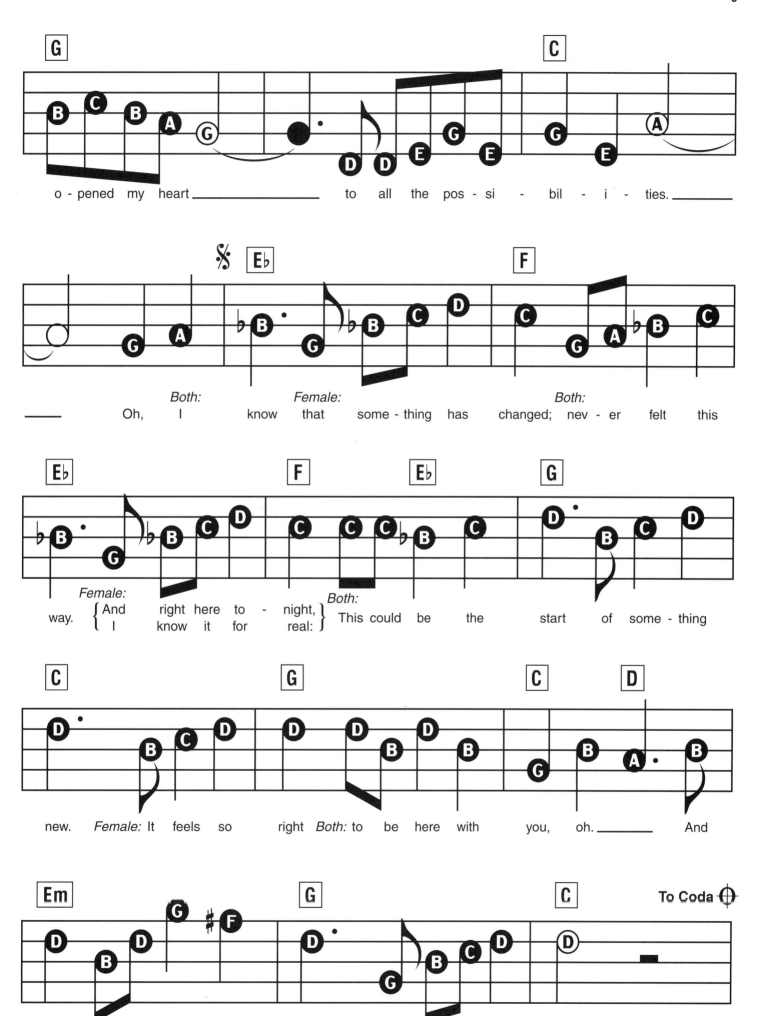

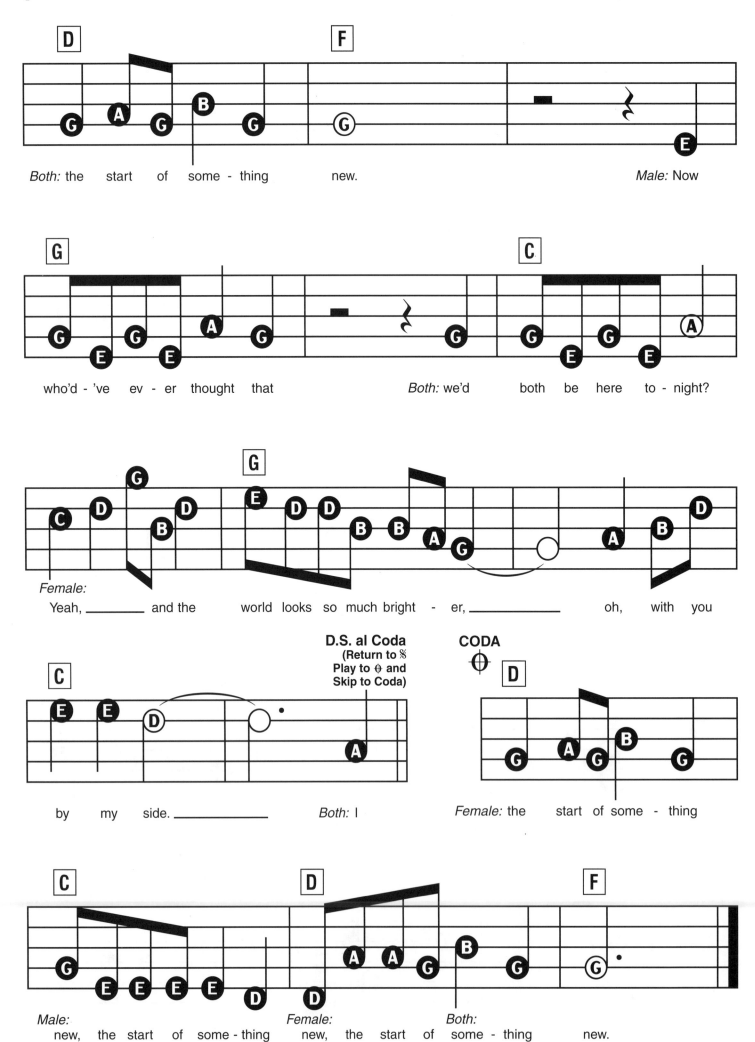

Get'cha Head in the Game

Registration 3
Rhythm: Dance, Funk or Rock

Words and Music by Ray Cham,
Greg Cham and Andrew Seeley

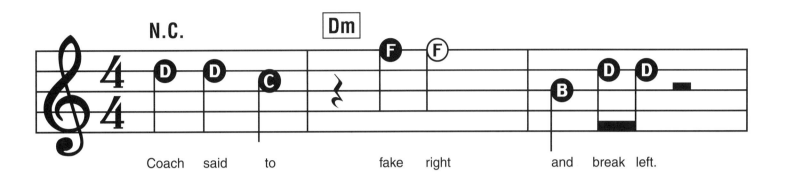

Coach said to fake right and break left.

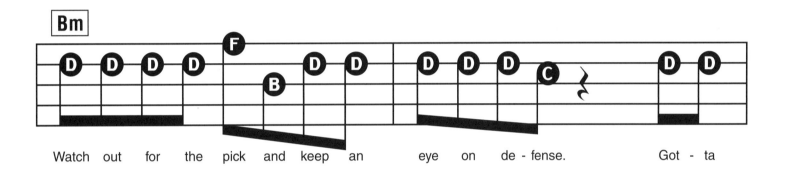

Watch out for the pick and keep an eye on de - fense. Got - ta

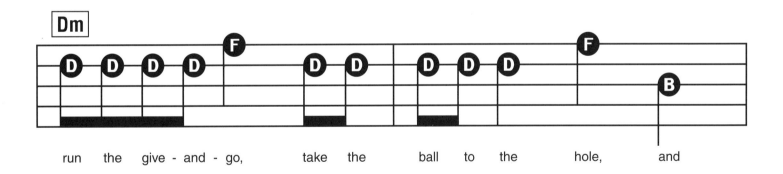

run the give - and - go, take the ball to the hole, and

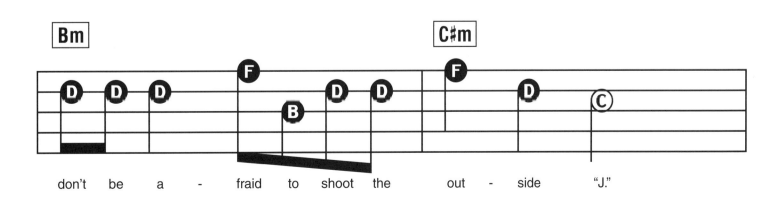

don't be a - fraid to shoot the out - side "J."

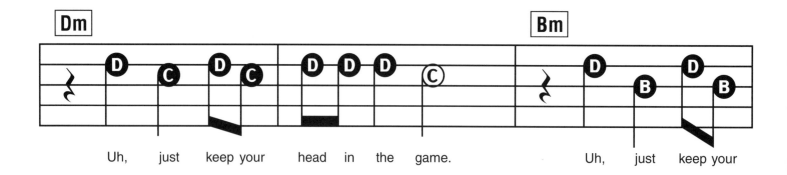

Uh, just keep your head in the game. Uh, just keep your

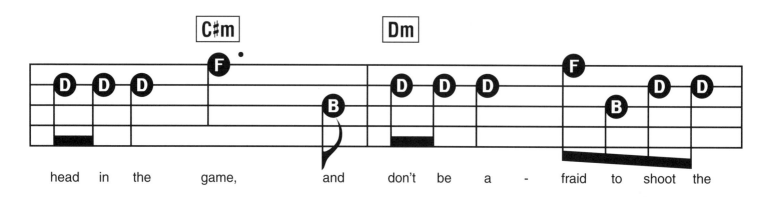

head in the game, and don't be a - fraid to shoot the

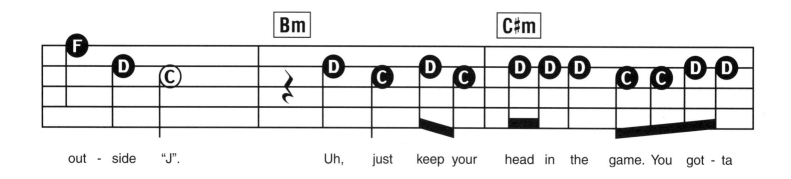

out - side "J". Uh, just keep your head in the game. You got - ta

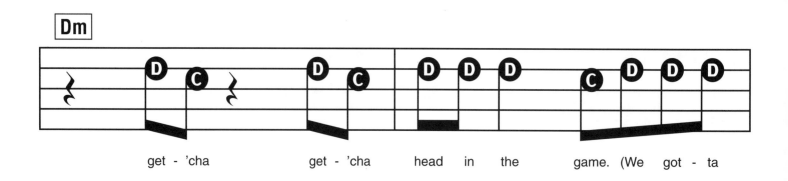

get - 'cha get - 'cha head in the game. (We got - ta

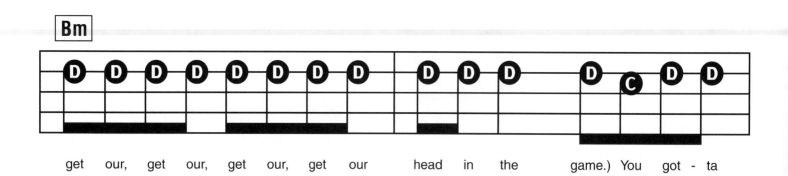

get our, get our, get our, get our head in the game.) You got - ta

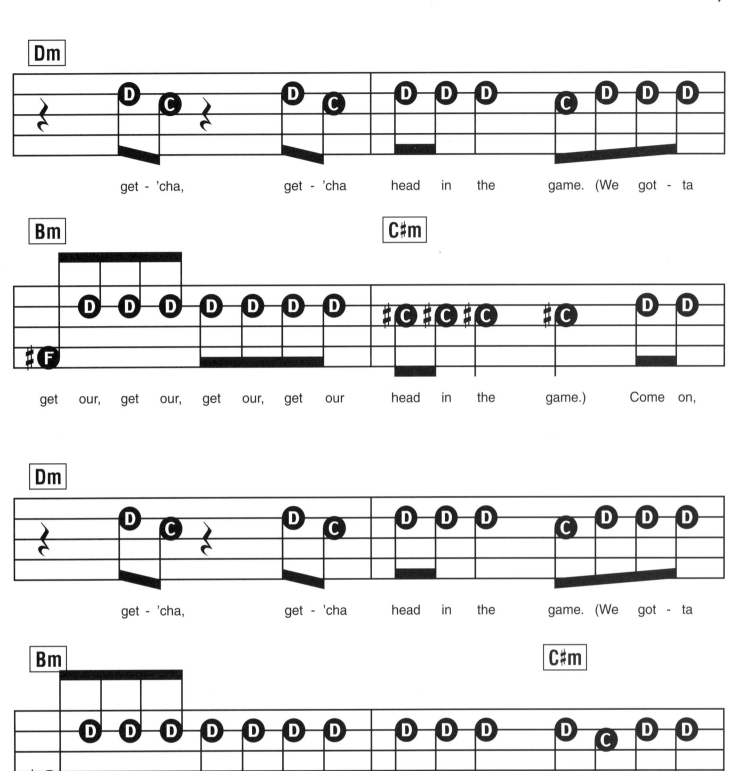

get - 'cha,   get - 'cha head in the game. (We got - ta

get our, get our, get our, get our head in the game.) Come on,

get - 'cha,   get - 'cha head in the game. (We got - ta

get our, get our, get our, get our head in the game.) You got - ta

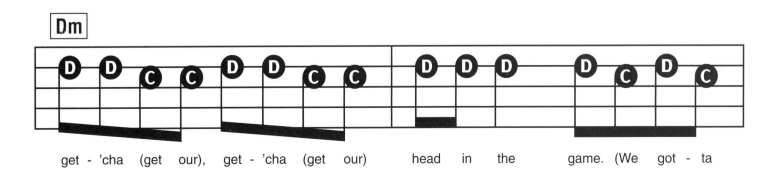

get - 'cha (get our), get - 'cha (get our) head in the game. (We got - ta

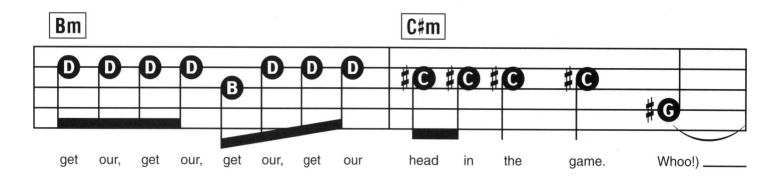

get our, get our, get our, get our head in the game. Whoo!) _____

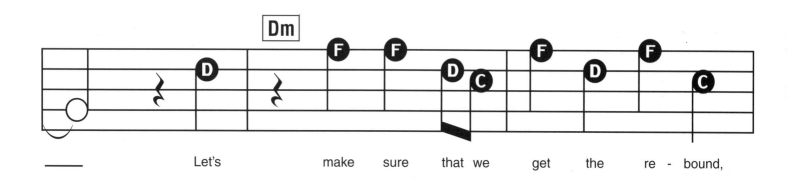

_____ Let's make sure that we get the re - bound,

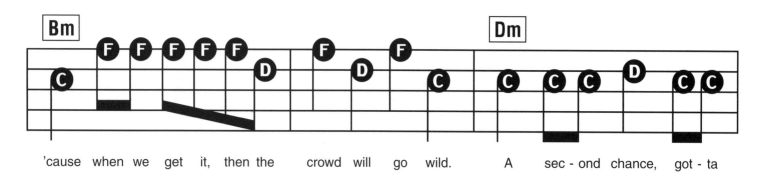

'cause when we get it, then the crowd will go wild. A sec - ond chance, got - ta

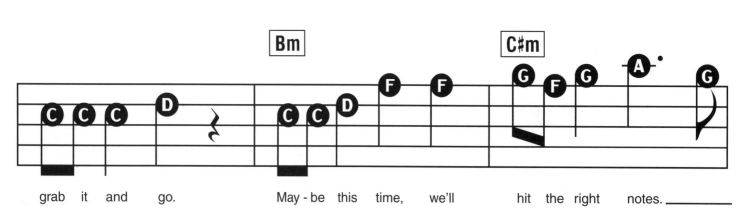

grab it and go. May - be this time, we'll hit the right notes. _____

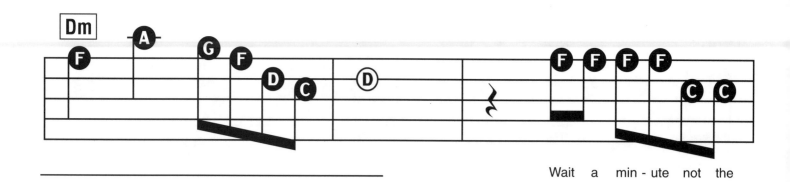

Wait a min - ute not the

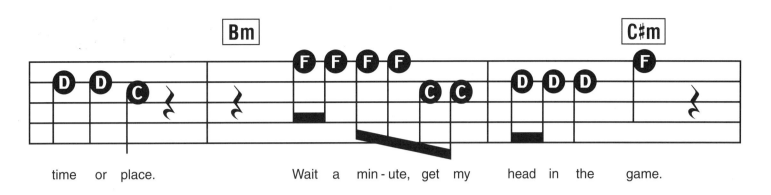

time or place. Wait a min-ute, get my head in the game.

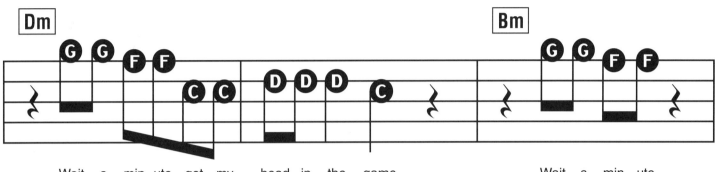

Wait a min-ute, get my head in the game. Wait a min-ute,

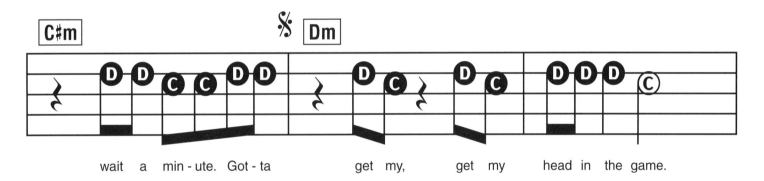

wait a min-ute. Got-ta get my, get my head in the game.

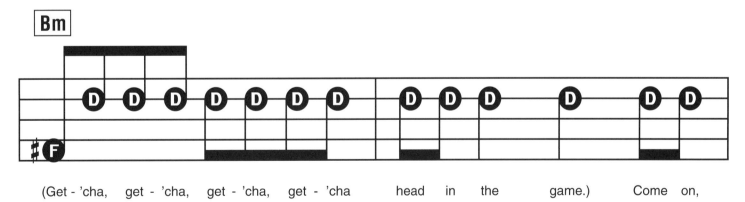

(Get-'cha, get-'cha, get-'cha, get-'cha head in the game.) Come on,

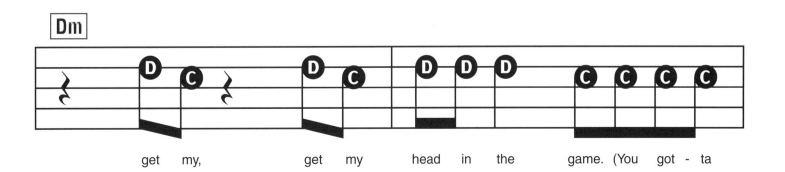

get my, get my head in the game. (You got-ta

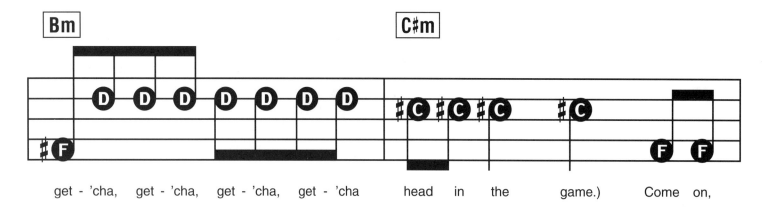

get - 'cha, get - 'cha, get - 'cha, get - 'cha head in the game.) Come on,

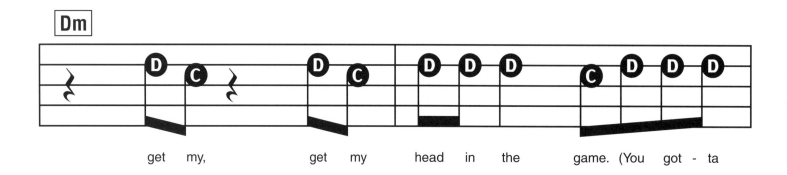

get my, get my head in the game. (You got - ta

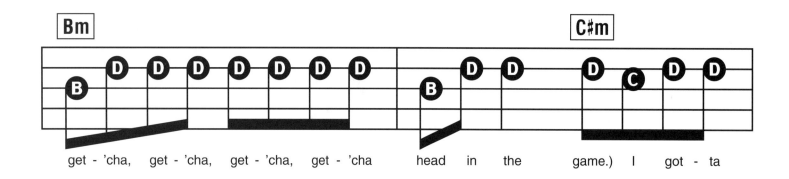

get - 'cha, get - 'cha, get - 'cha, get - 'cha head in the game.) I got - ta

To Coda ⊕

get my (get - 'cha), get my (get - 'cha) head in the game. (You got - ta

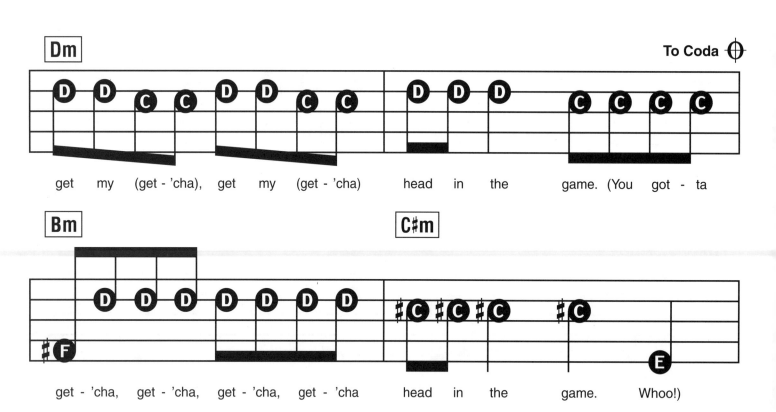

get - 'cha, get - 'cha, get - 'cha, get - 'cha head in the game. Whoo!)

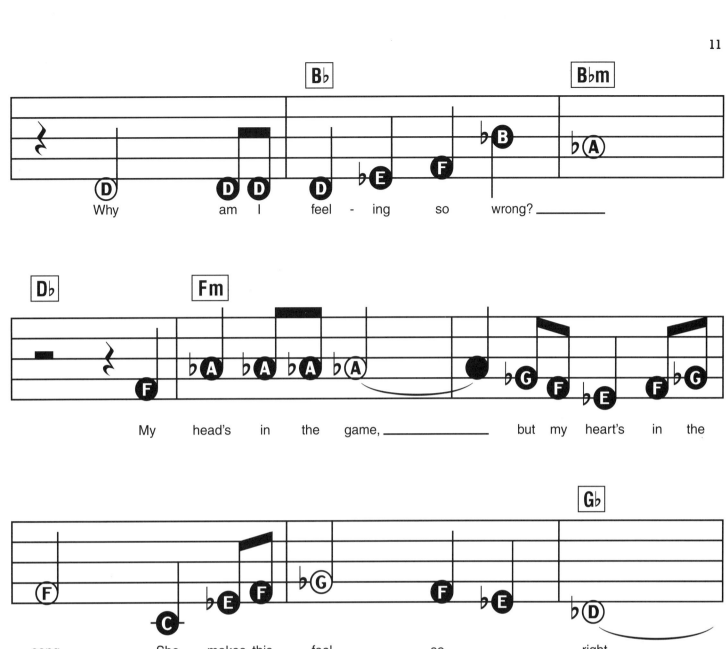

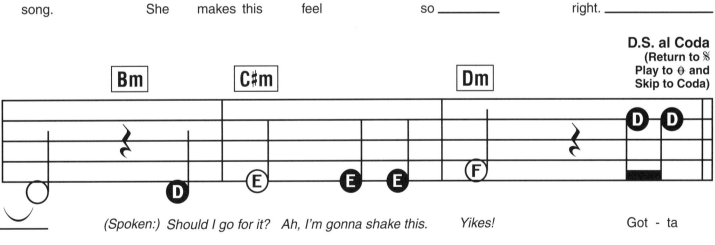

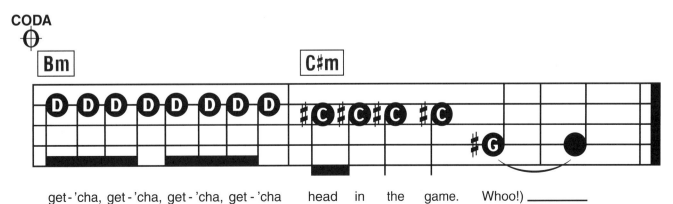

What I've Been Looking For

Registration 8
Rhythm: Pop or Rock

Words and Music by Andy Dodd
and Adam Watts

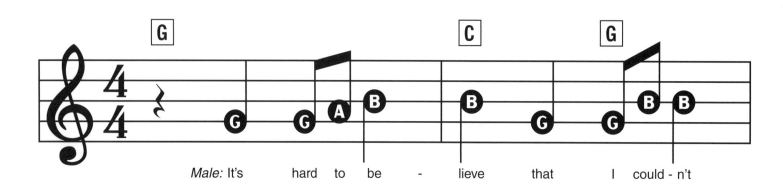

Male: It's hard to be - lieve that I could-n't

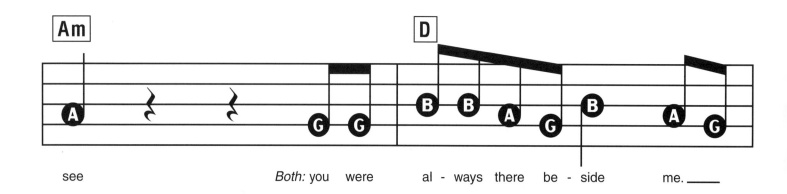

see   Both: you were al - ways there be - side me. ____

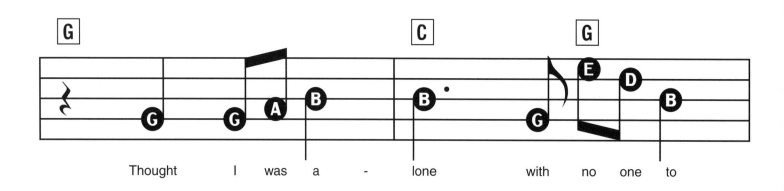

Thought I was a - lone with no one to

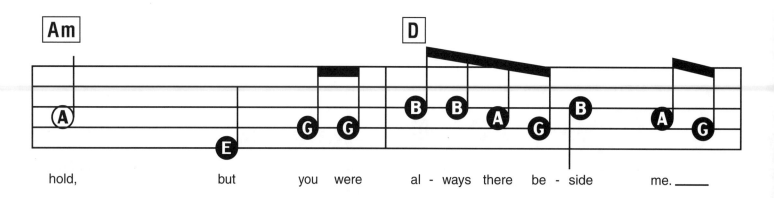

hold, but you were al - ways there be - side me. ____

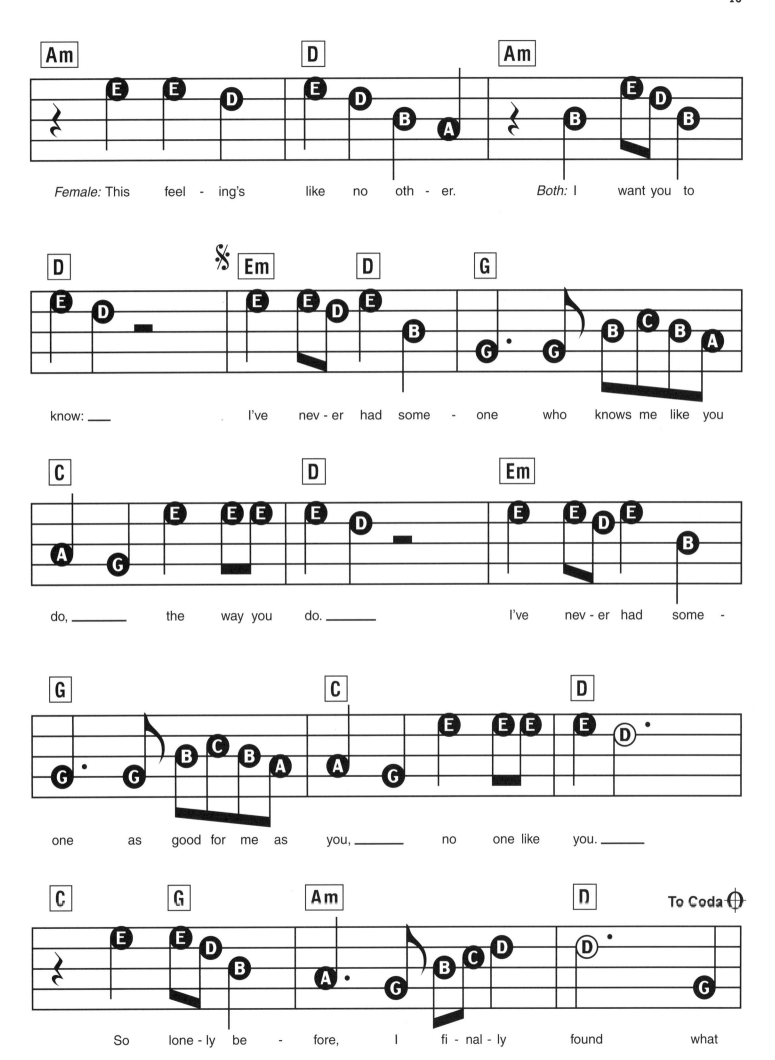

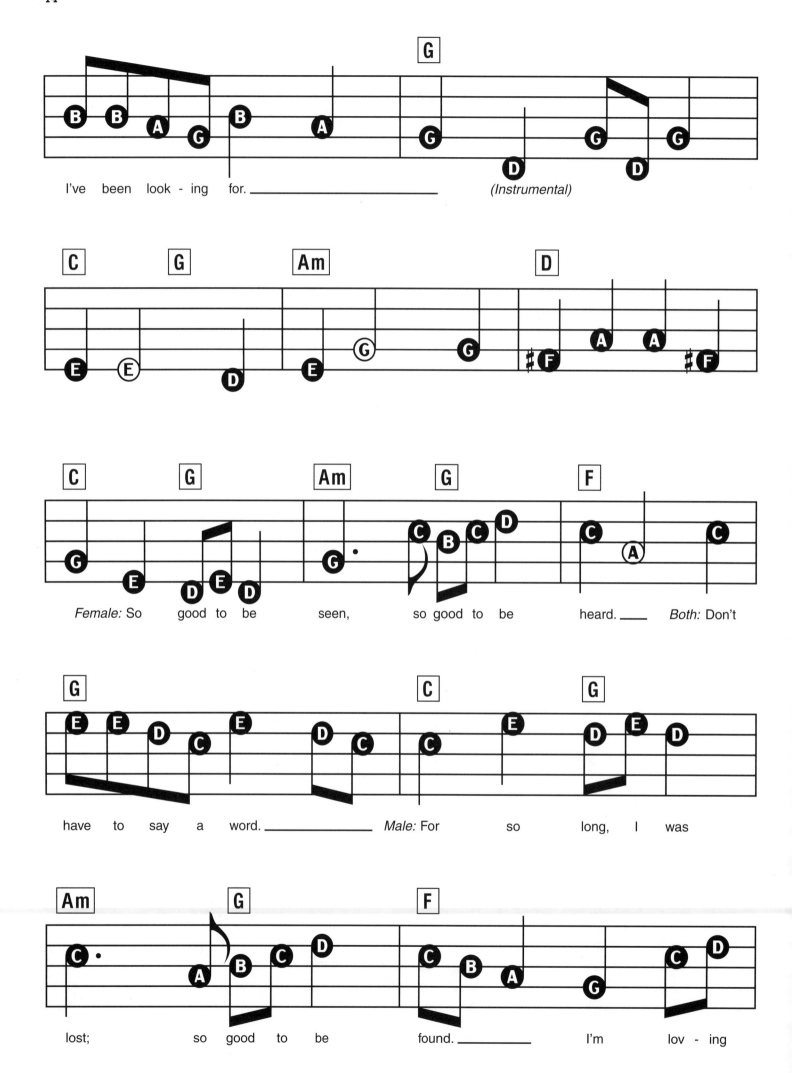

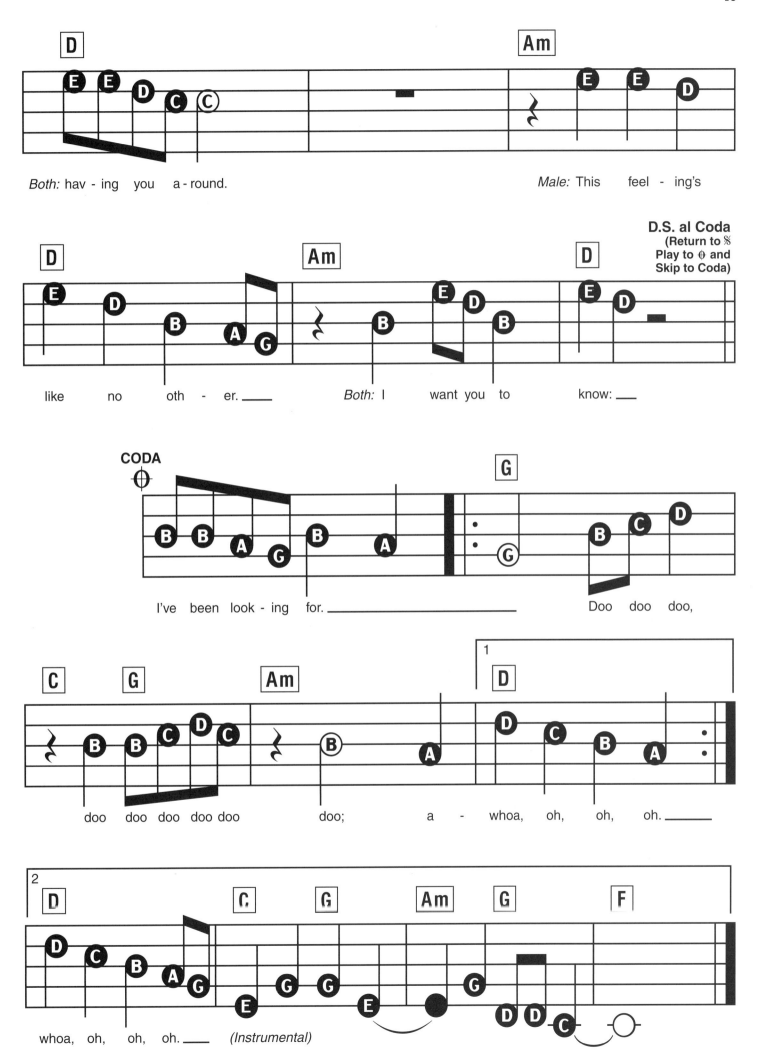

Stick to the Status Quo

Registration 4
Rhythm: Dance or Rock

Words and Music by David N. Lawrence
and Faye Greenberg

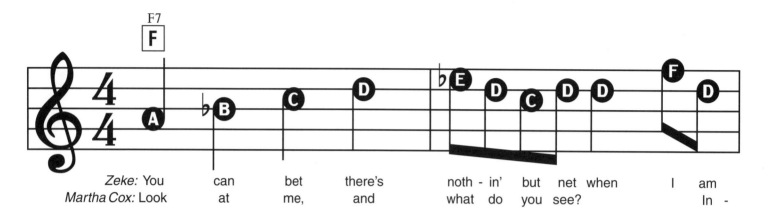

Zeke: You can bet there's noth-in' but net when I am
Martha Cox: Look at me, and what do you see? In -

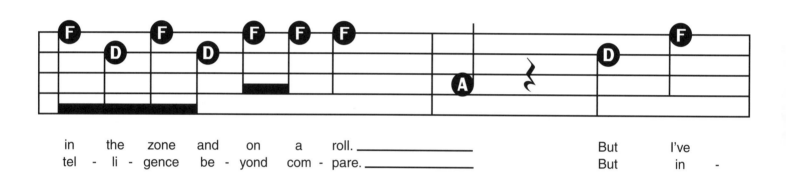

in the zone and on a roll._____ But I've
tel - li - gence be - yond com - pare._____ But in -

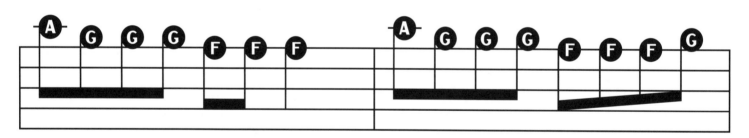

got a con - fes - sion, my own se - cret ob - ses - sion, and it's mak -
side, I am stir - ing; some - thing strange is oc - cur - ring. It's a se -

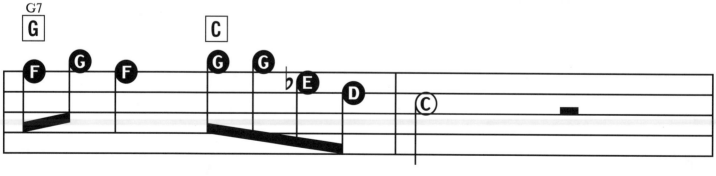

ing me ____ lose con - trol. _____
cret I ____ need to share. _____

Jocks: Ev - 'ry - bod - y, _____ gath - er _____ 'round.
Brainiacs: O - pen _____ up, dig _____ way down _____ deep.

Zeke: If Troy can tell his secret, then I can tell mine… I bake. Jock 1: What?!
Martha: Hip-hop is my passion! I love to pop, and lock, and jam, and break!

1st time only

Zeke: I love to bake! Strudels, scones, even apple pandowdy!
Brainiac 1: Is that even legal?

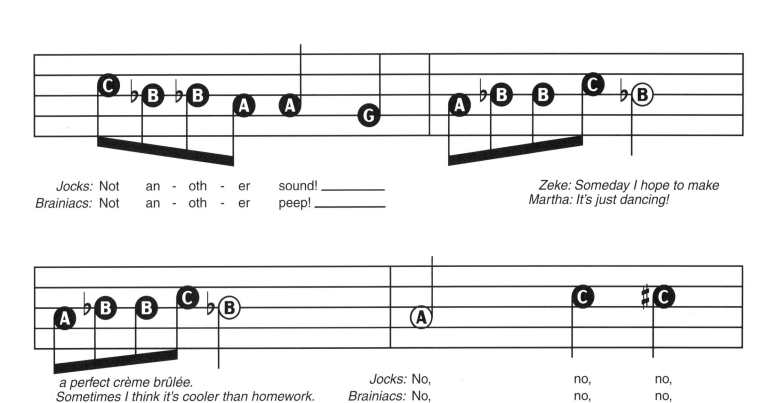

Jocks: Not an - oth - er sound! _____ Zeke: Someday I hope to make
Brainiacs: Not an - oth - er peep! _____ Martha: It's just dancing!

a perfect crème brûlée. Jocks: No, no, no,
Sometimes I think it's cooler than homework. Brainiacs: No, no, no,

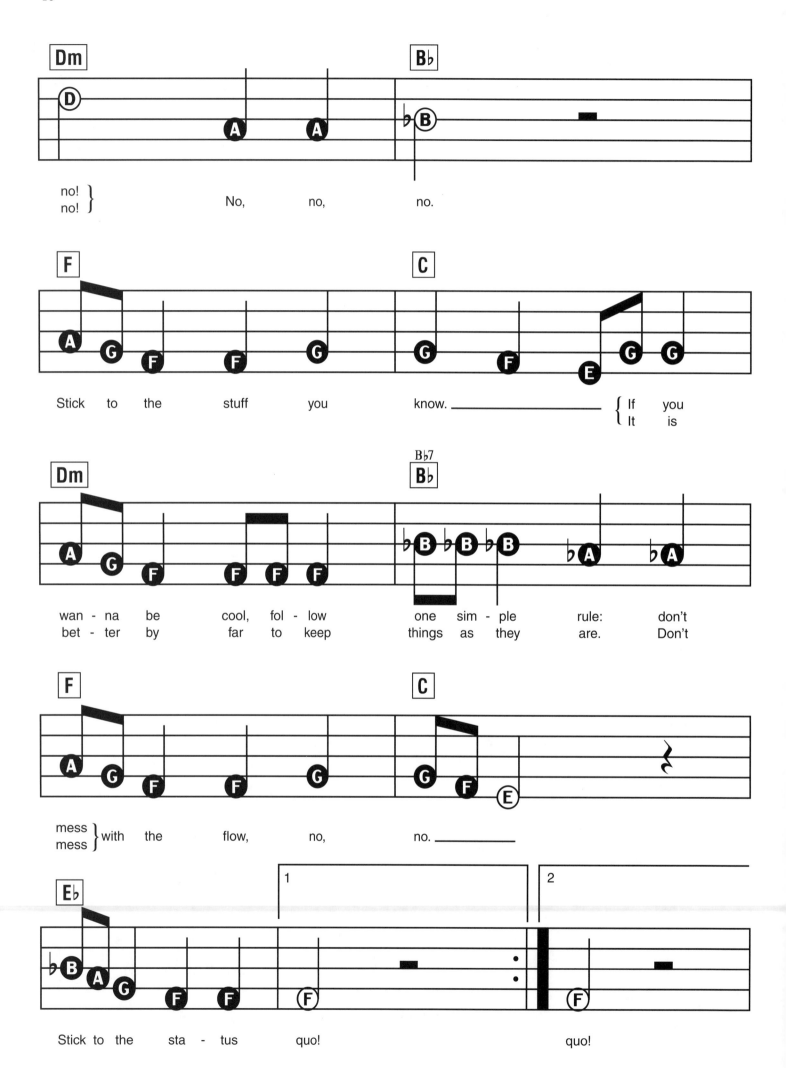

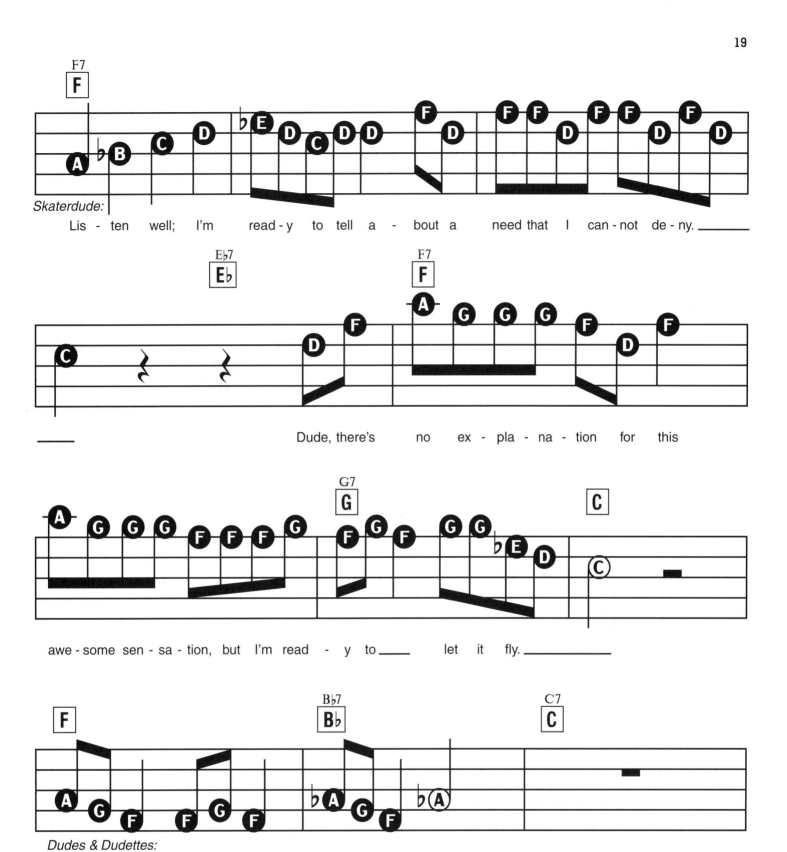

Skaterdude:
Lis - ten well; I'm read - y to tell a - bout a need that I can - not de - ny. _____

_____ Dude, there's no ex - pla - na - tion for this

awe - some sen - sa - tion, but I'm read - y to ____ let it fly. _____

Dudes & Dudettes:
Speak your ____ mind and ____ you'll be ____ heard.   [dialogue continues]

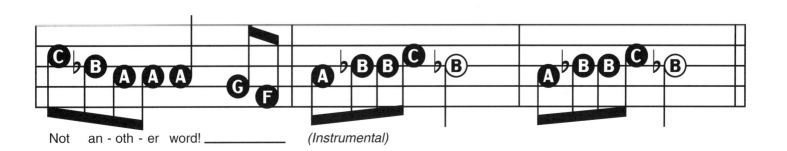

Not an - oth - er word! _____   (Instrumental)

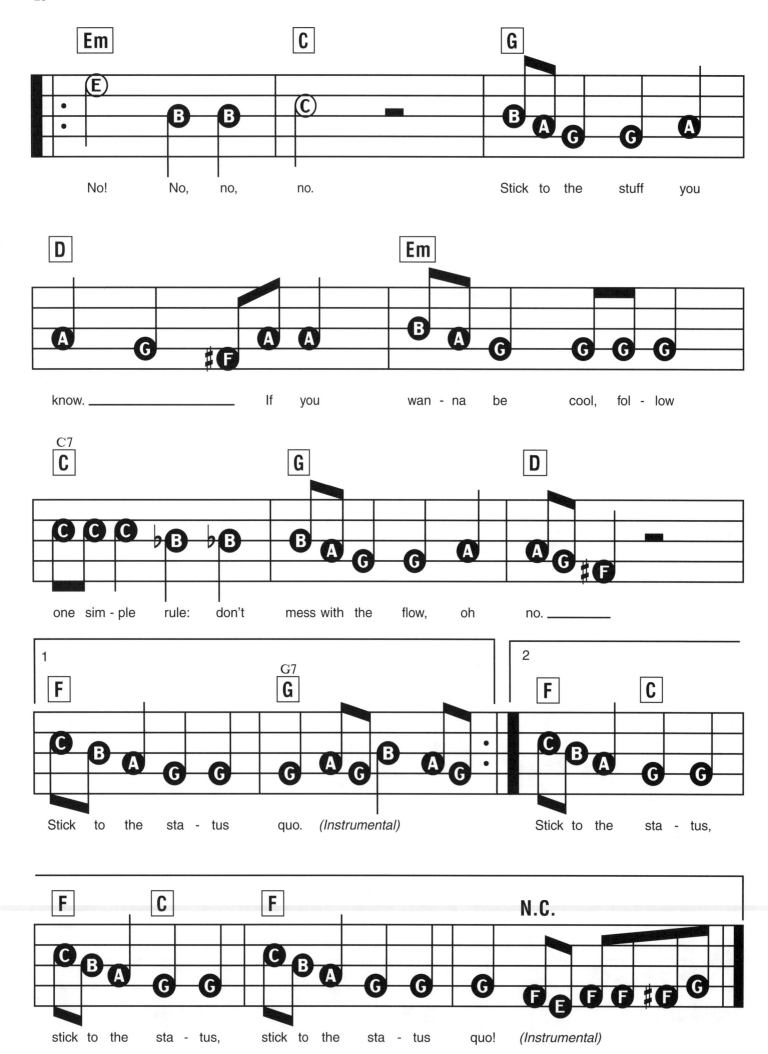

When There Was Me and You

Registration 2
Rhythm: 4/4 Ballad or 8 Beat

Words and Music by
Jamie Houston

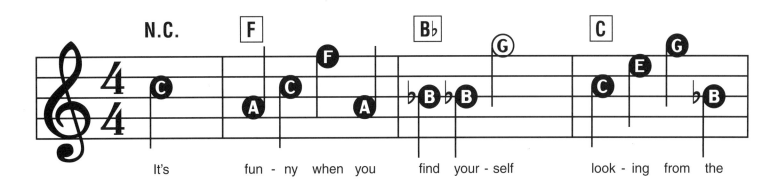

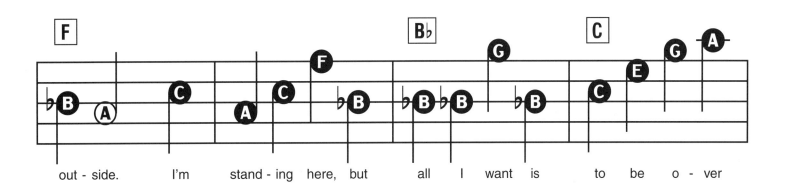

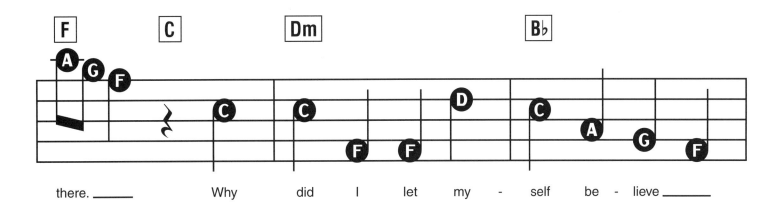

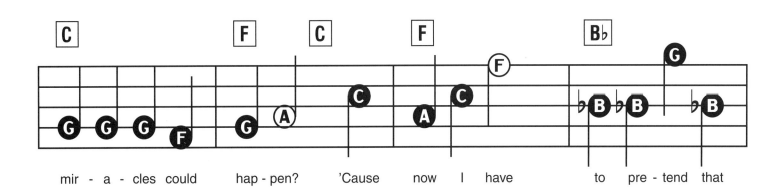

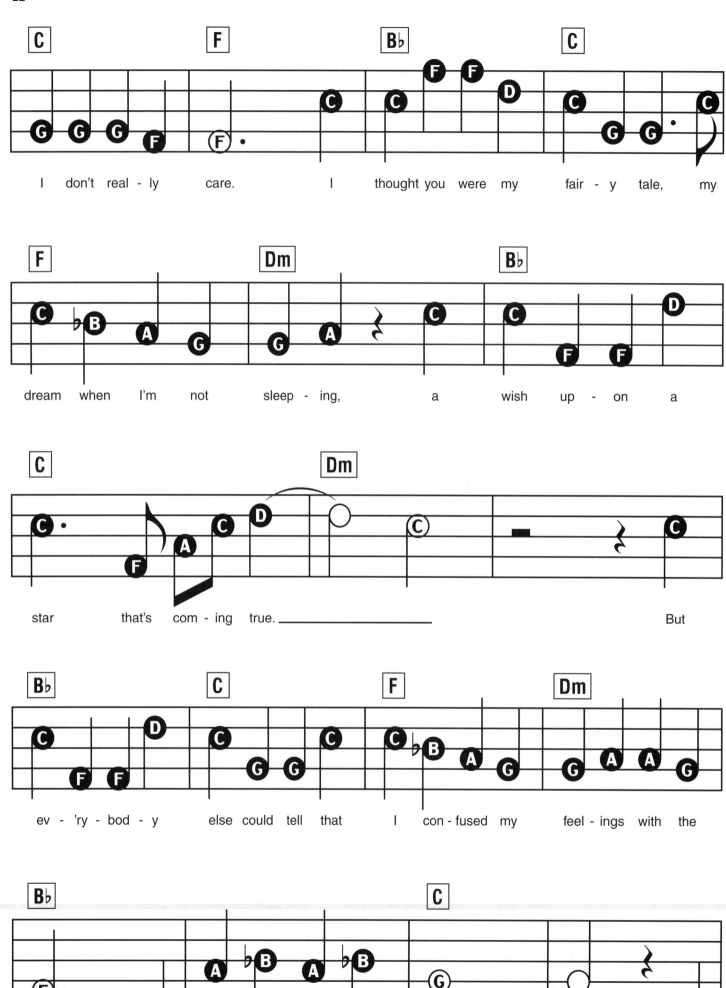

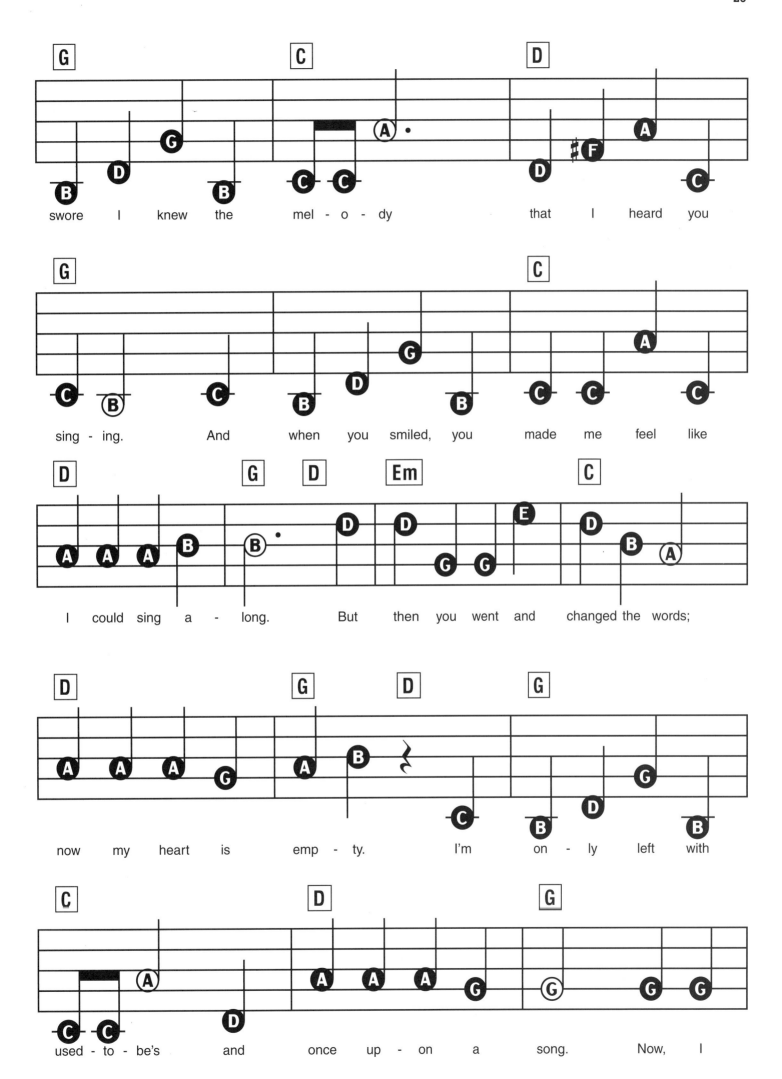

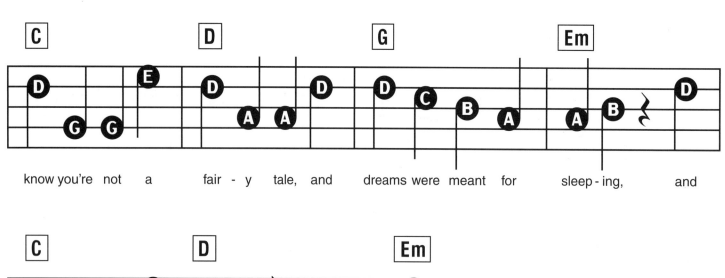

know you're not a fair - y tale, and dreams were meant for sleep - ing, and

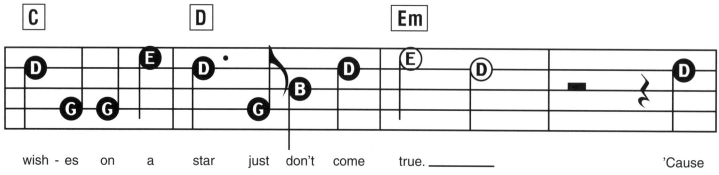

wish - es on a star just don't come true. _____ 'Cause

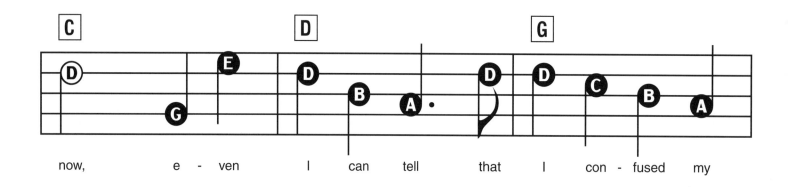

now, e - ven I can tell that I con - fused my

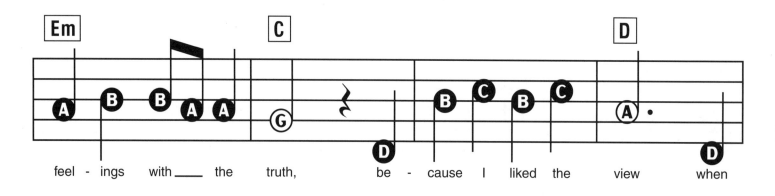

feel - ings with ___ the truth, be - cause I liked the view when

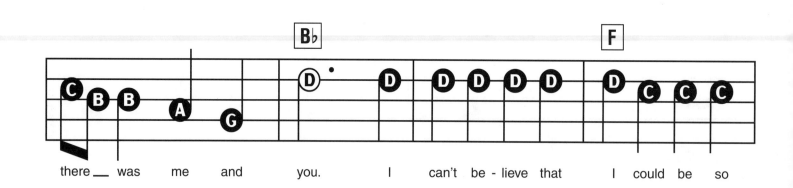

there ___ was me and you. I can't be - lieve that I could be so

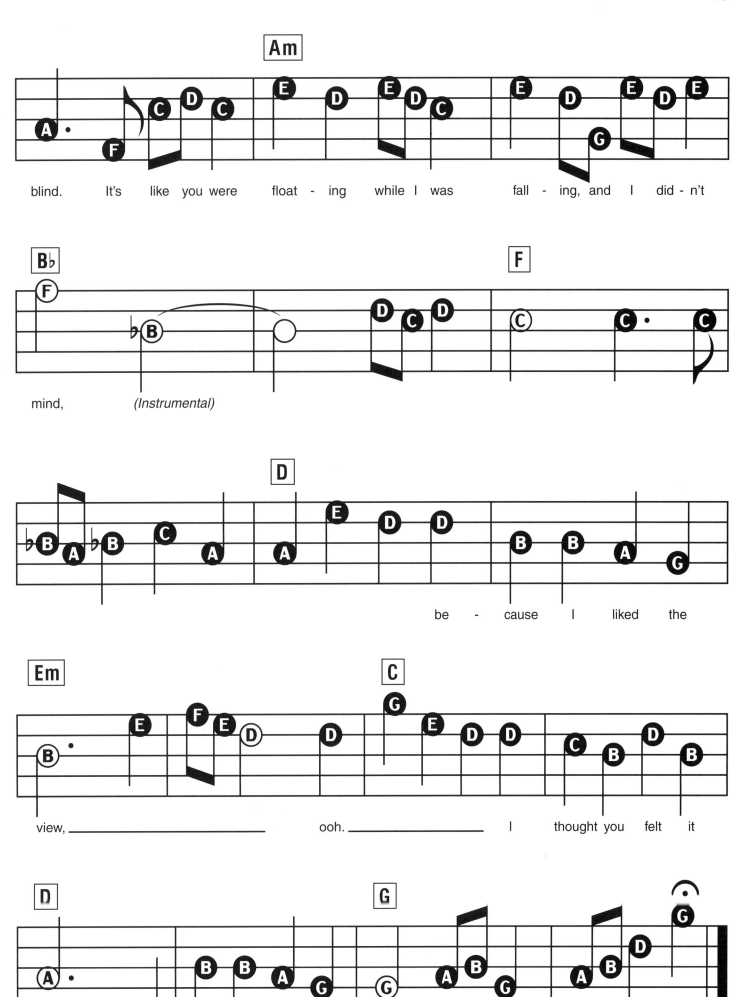

Bop to the Top

Registration 4
Rhythm: Samba or Rock

Words and Music by Randy Petersen
and Kevin Quinn

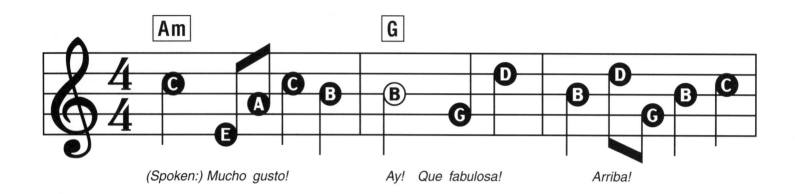

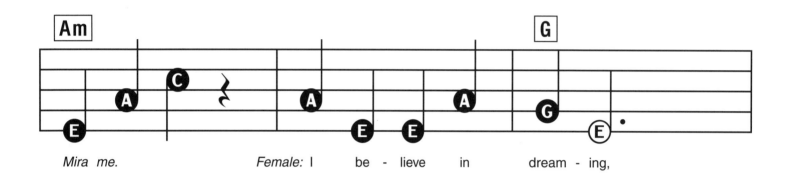

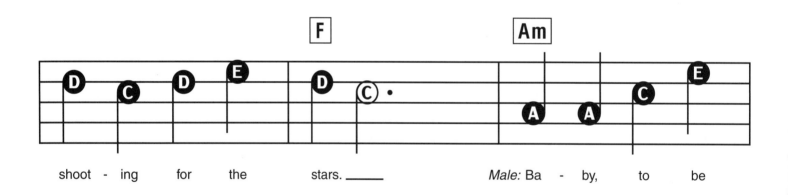

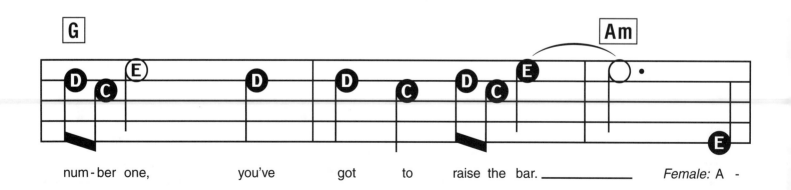

27

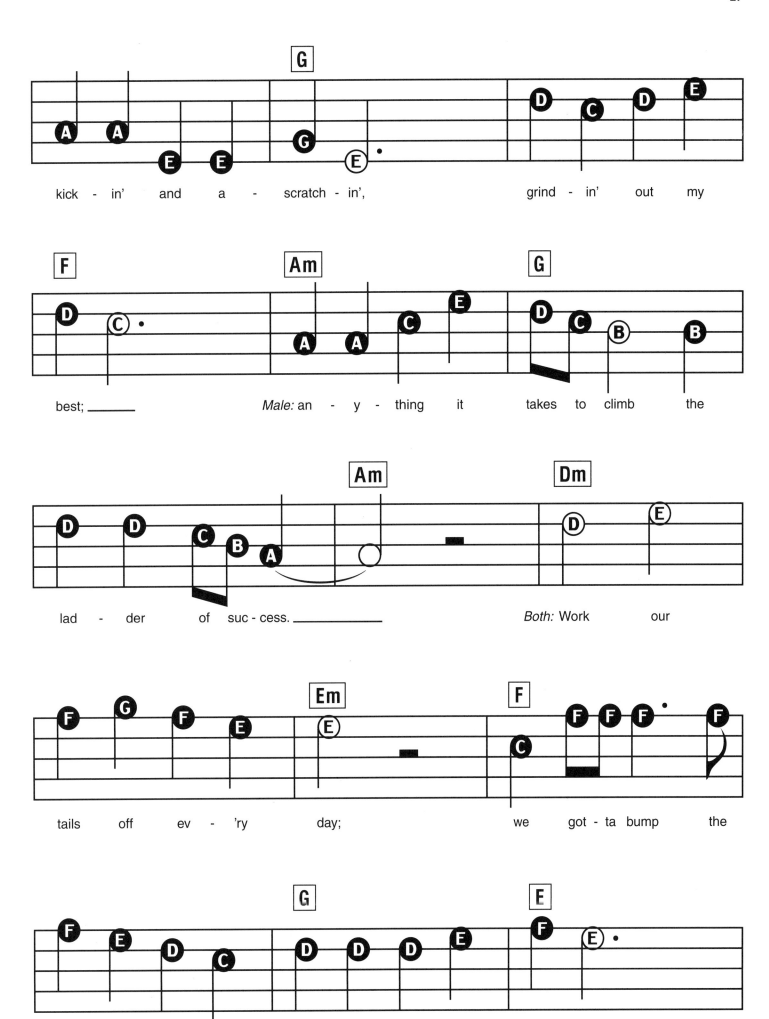

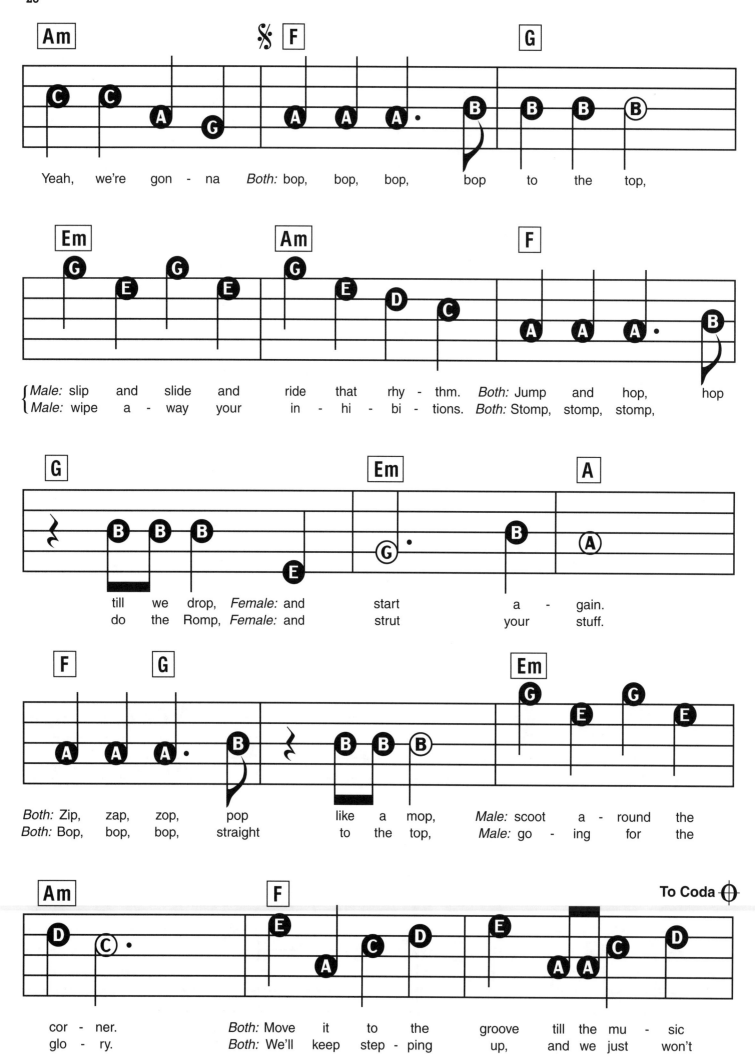

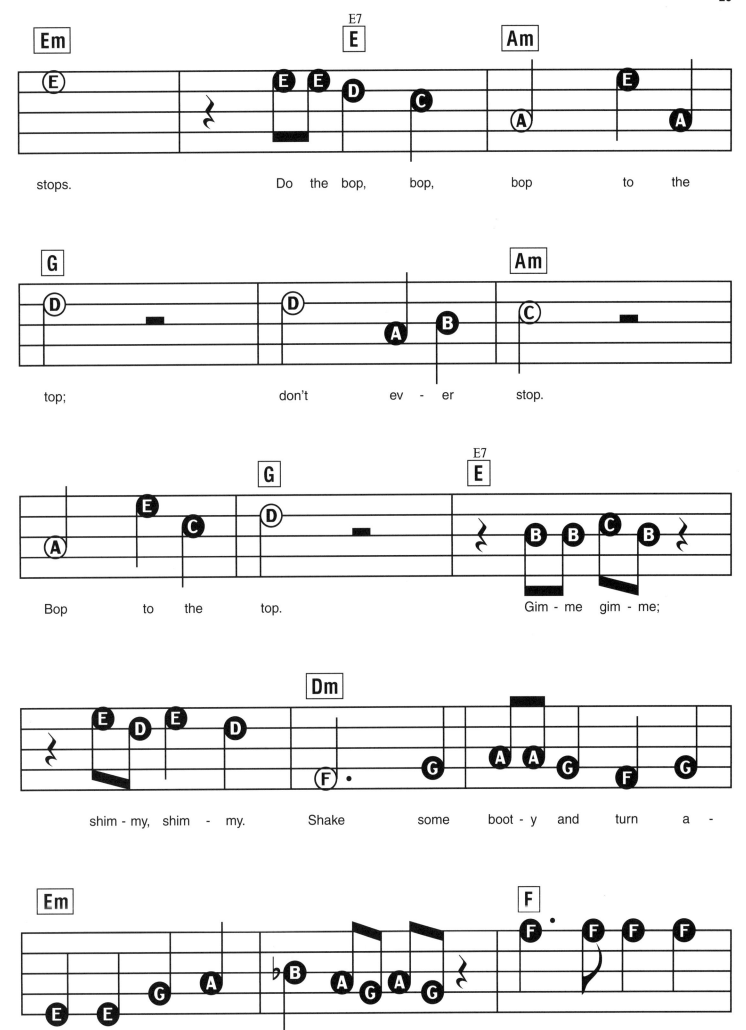

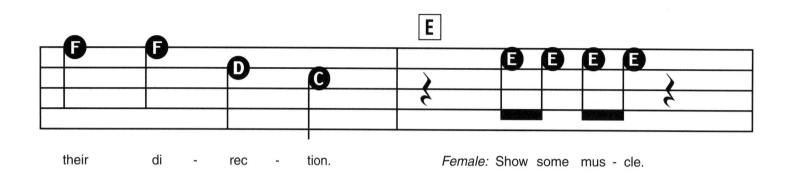

their di - rec - tion. *Female:* Show some mus - cle.

D.S. al Coda
(Return to ％
Play to ⊕ and
Skip to Coda)

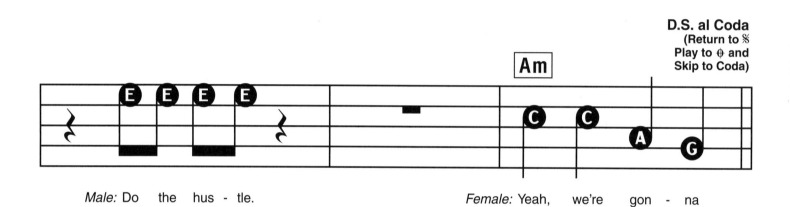

Male: Do the hus - tle. *Female:* Yeah, we're gon - na

CODA

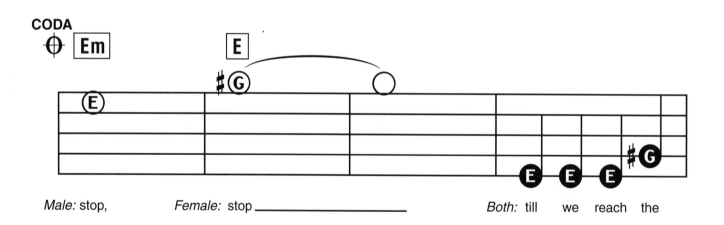

Male: stop, *Female:* stop _____ *Both:* till we reach the

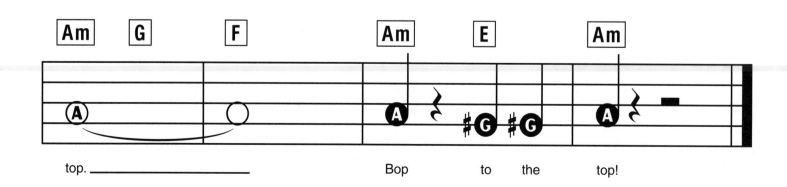

top. _____ Bop to the top!

We're All in This Together

Registration 4
Rhythm: Dance or 8 Beat

Words and Music by Matthew Gerrard
and Robbie Nevil

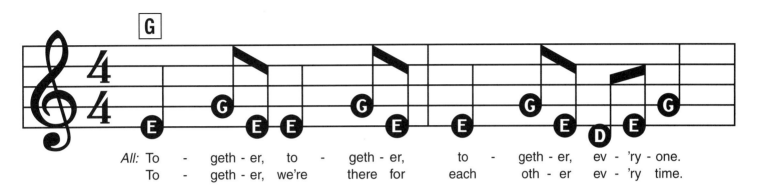

All: To - geth - er, to - geth - er, to - geth - er, ev - 'ry - one.
To - geth - er, we're there for each oth - er ev - 'ry time.

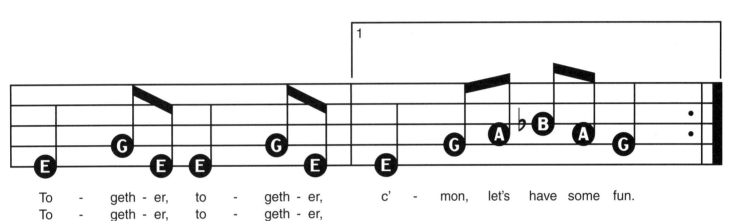

To - geth - er, to - geth - er, c' - mon, let's have some fun.
To - geth - er, to - geth - er,

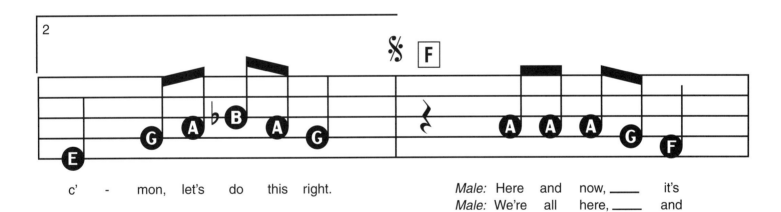

c' - mon, let's do this right.
Male: Here and now,____ it's
Male: We're all here,____ and

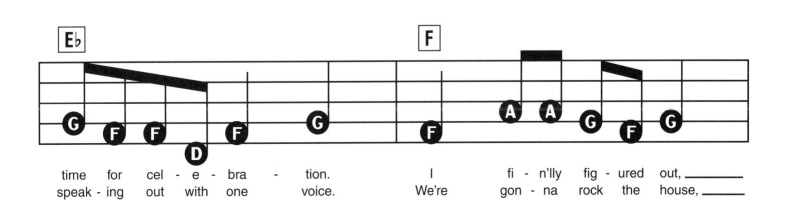

time for cel - e - bra - tion. I fi - n'lly fig - ured out,_____
speak - ing out with one voice. We're gon - na rock the house,_____

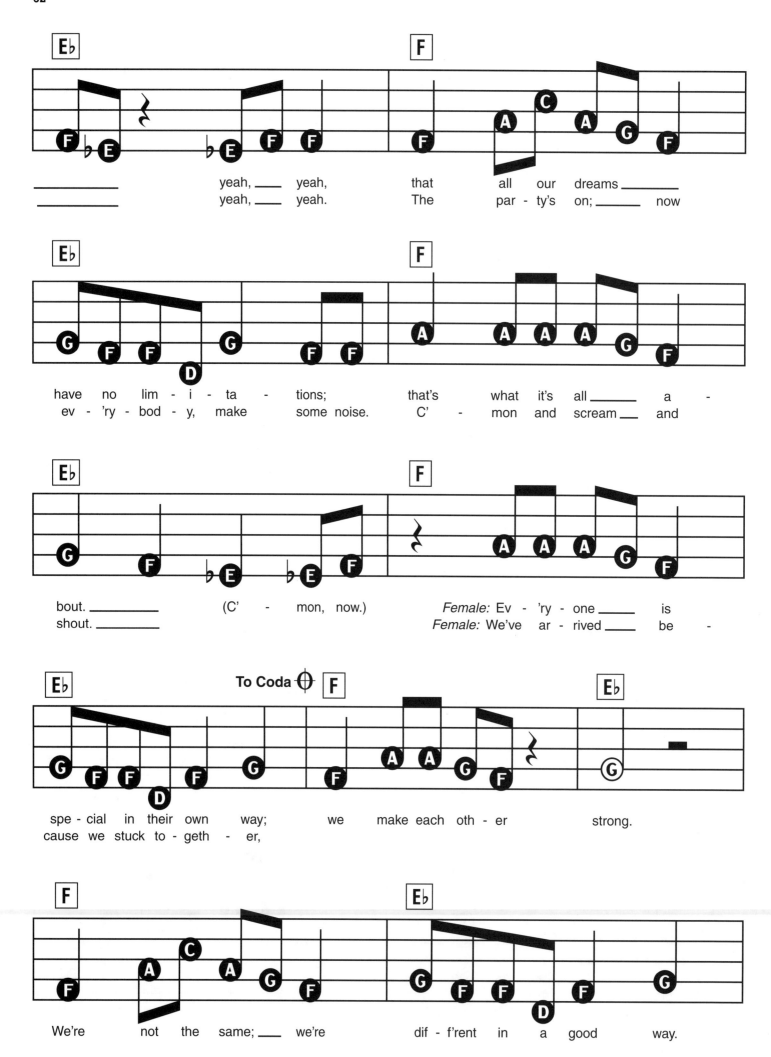

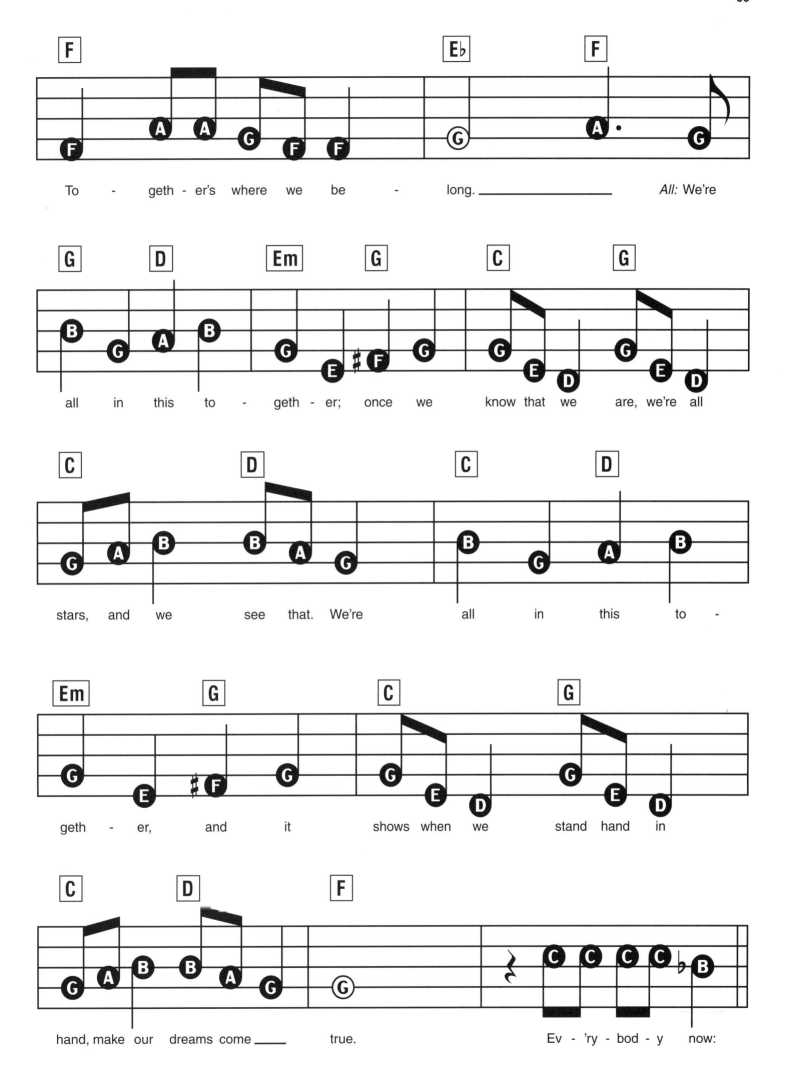

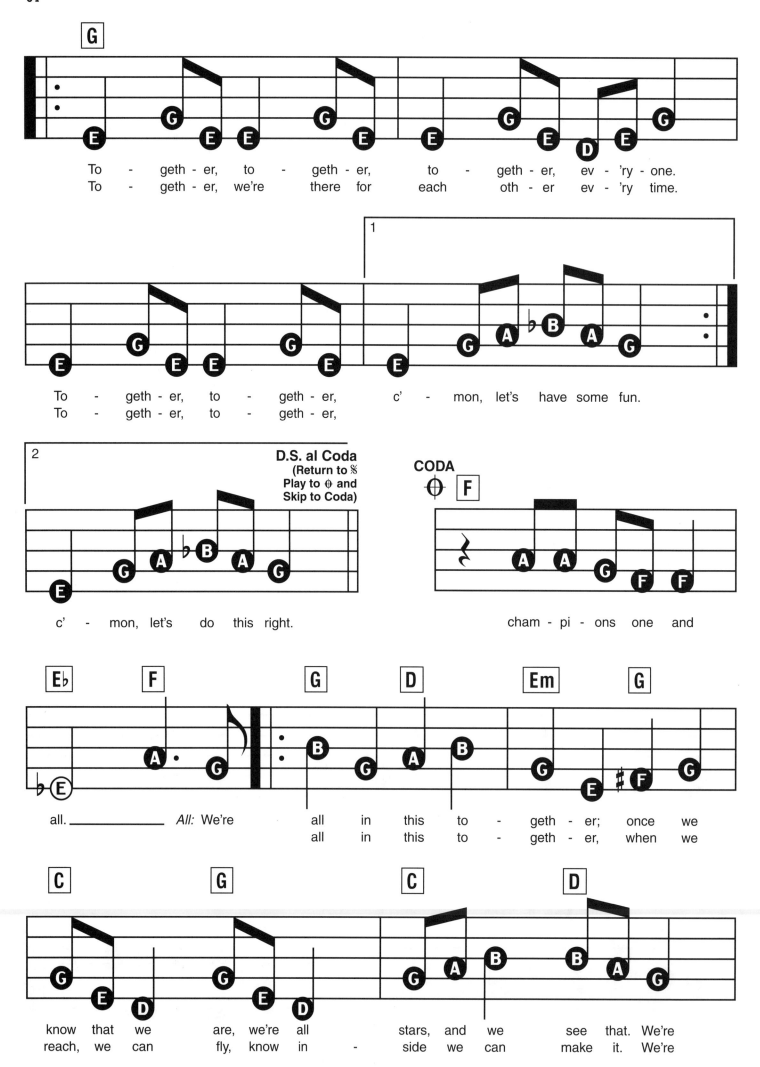

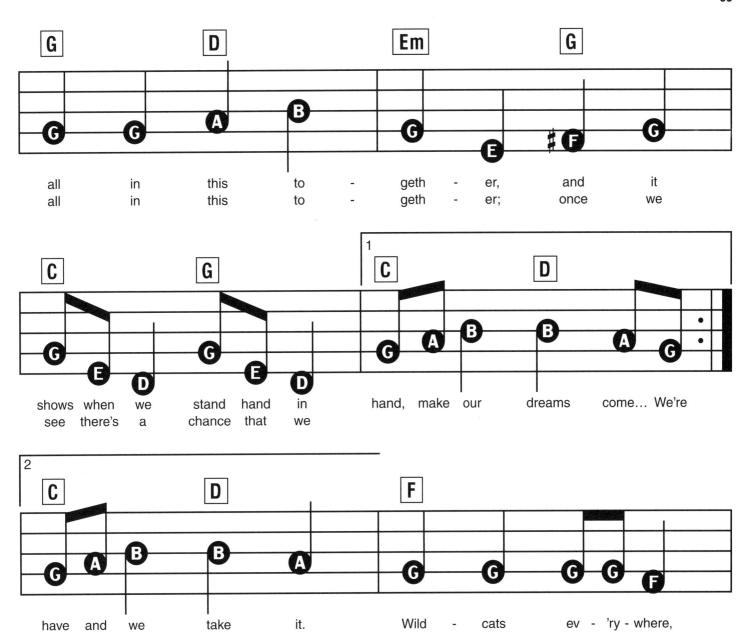

all in this to - geth - er, and it
all in this to - geth - er; once we

shows when we stand hand in
see there's a chance that we

hand, make our dreams come... We're

have and we take it. Wild - cats ev - 'ry - where,

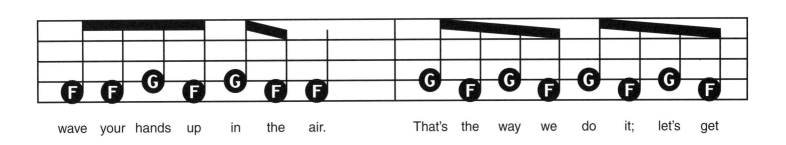

wave your hands up in the air. That's the way we do it; let's get

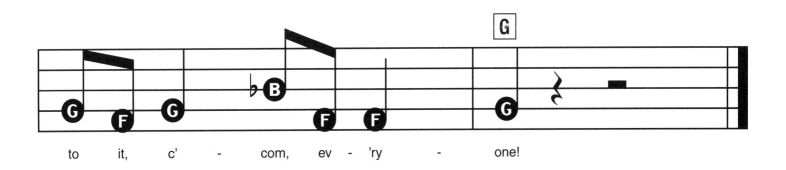

to it, c' - com, ev - 'ry - one!

Breaking Free

Registration 4
Rhythm: 8 Beat or Rock

Words and Music by
Jamie Houston

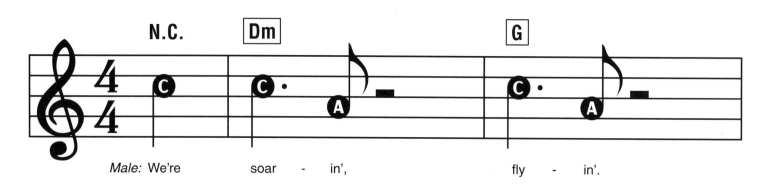

Male: We're soar - in', fly - in'.

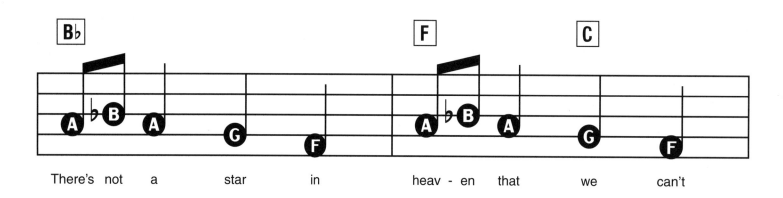

There's not a star in heav - en that we can't

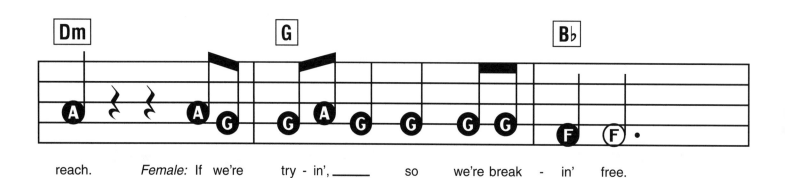

reach. Female: If we're try - in', _____ so we're break - in' free.

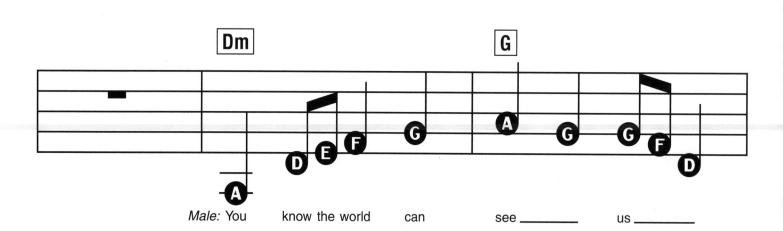

Male: You know the world can see _____ us _____

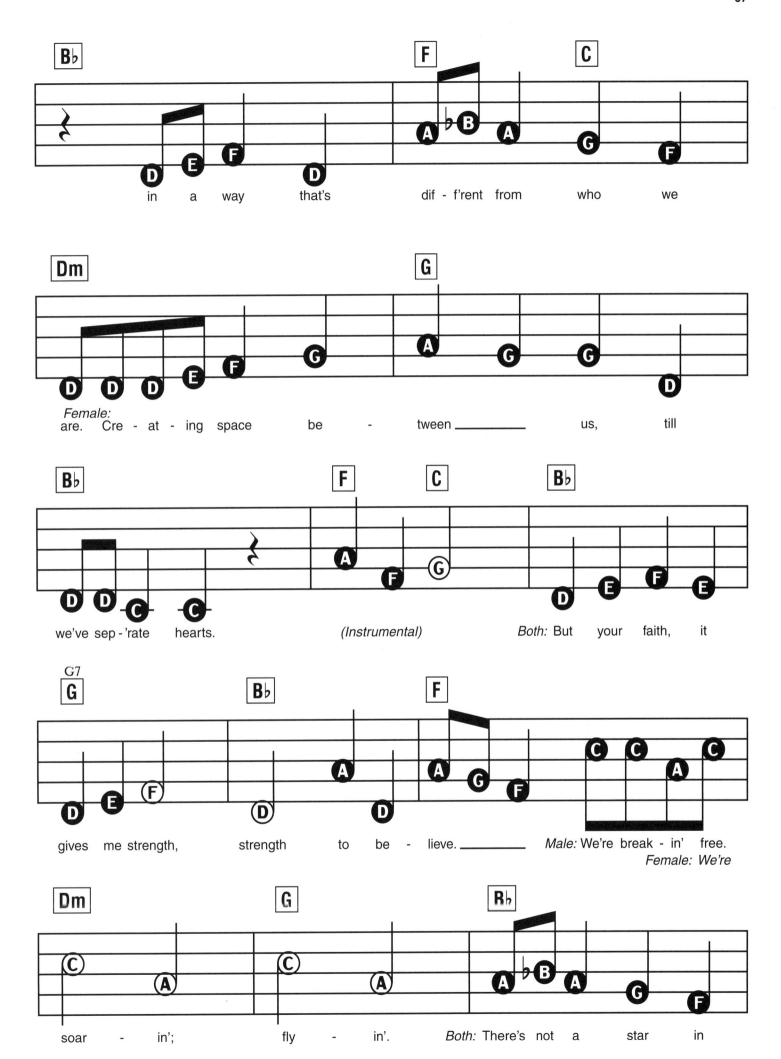

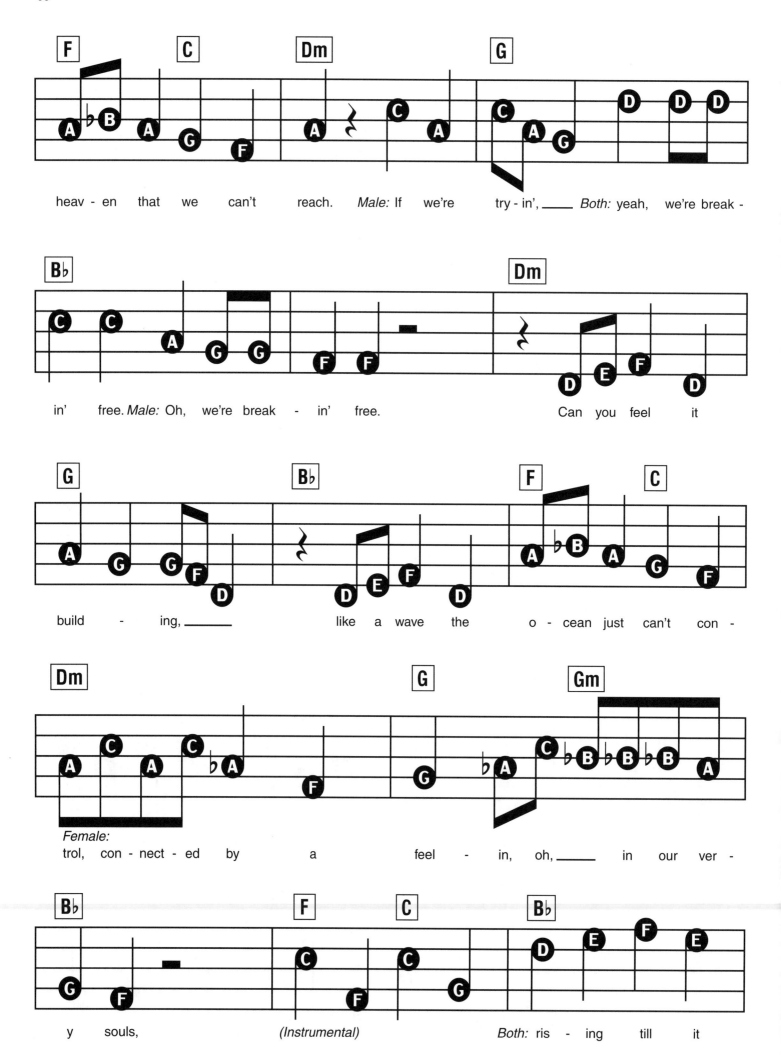

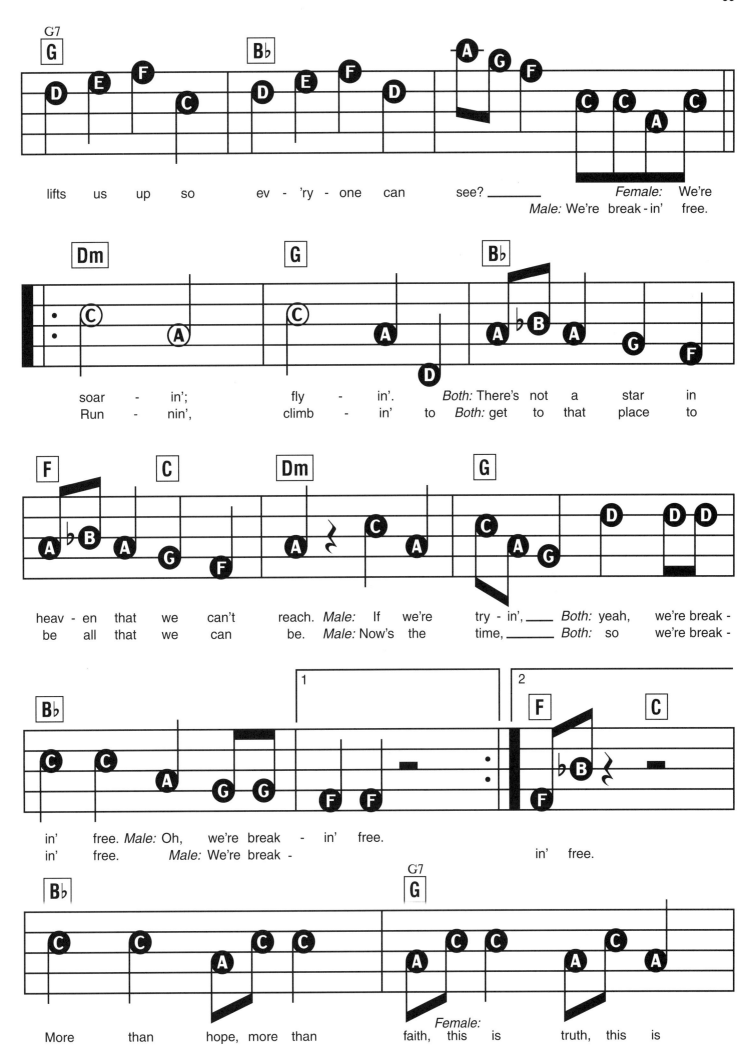

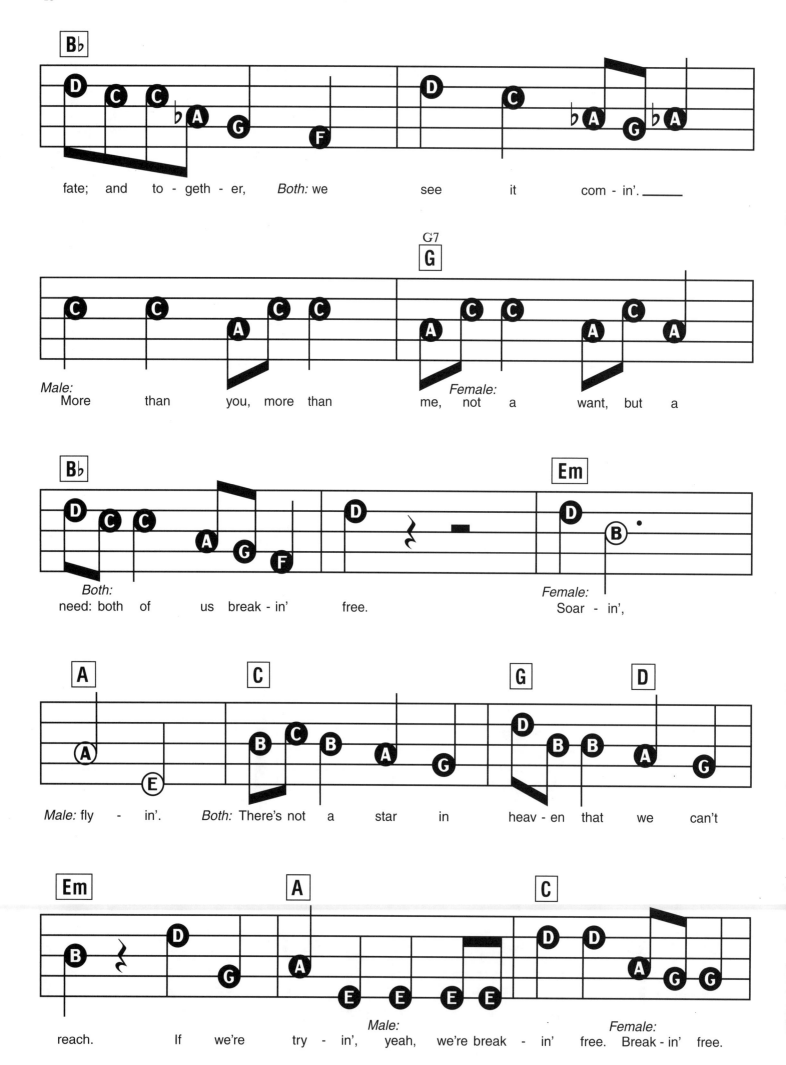

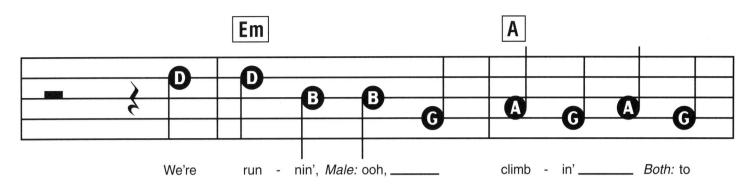

We're   run - nin', *Male:* ooh, _____   climb - in' _____ *Both:* to

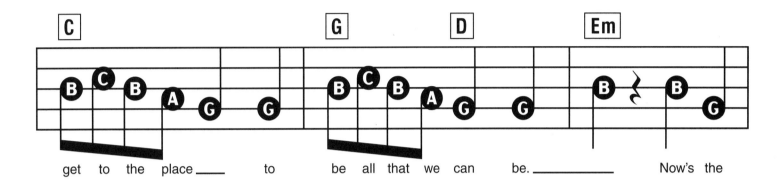

get   to   the   place ____   to   be   all   that   we   can   be. _____   Now's   the

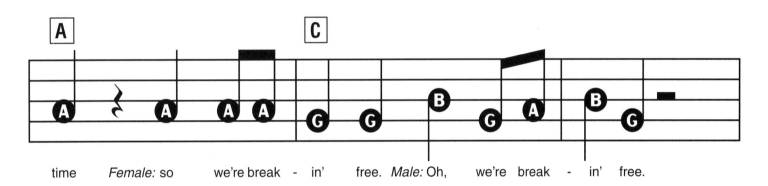

time   *Female:* so   we're break - in'   free. *Male:* Oh,   we're break - in'   free.

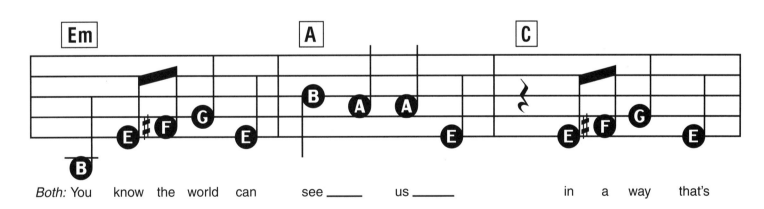

Both: You   know   the   world   can   see ____   us ____   in   a   way   that's

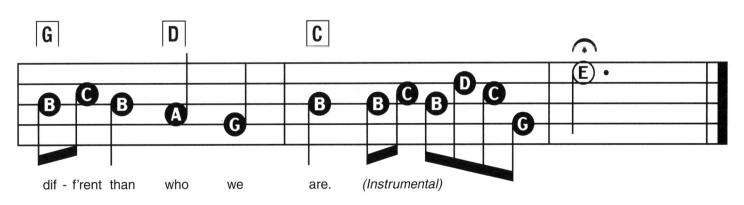

dif - f'rent than   who   we   are.   *(Instrumental)*

I Can't Take My Eyes Off of You

Registration 2
Rhythm: Latin Rock or Rock

Words and Music by Matthew Gerrard
and Robbie Nevil

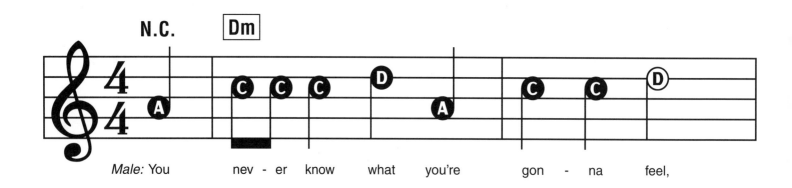

Male: You nev - er know what you're gon - na feel,

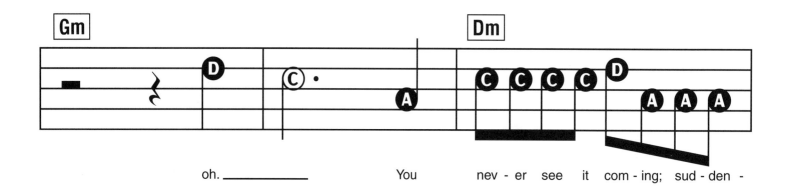

oh. _____ You nev - er see it com - ing; sud - den -

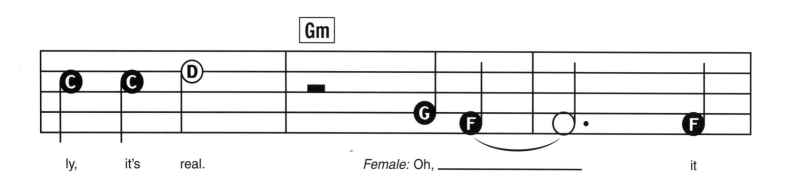

ly, it's real. *Female:* Oh, _____ it

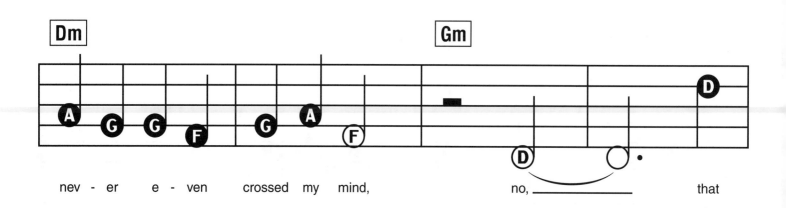

nev - er e - ven crossed my mind, no, _____ that

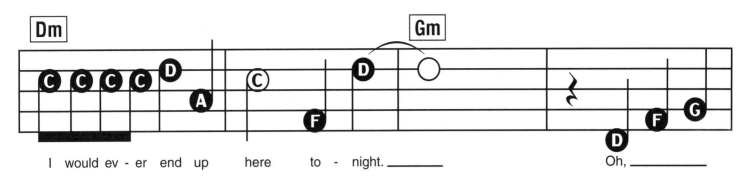

I would ev - er end up here to - night. _____ Oh, _____

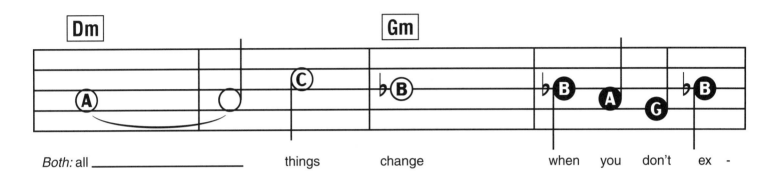

Both: all _____ things change when you don't ex -

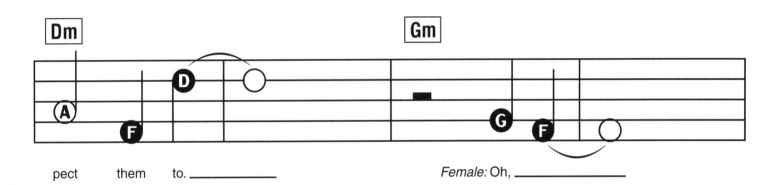

pect them to. _____ *Female:* Oh, _____

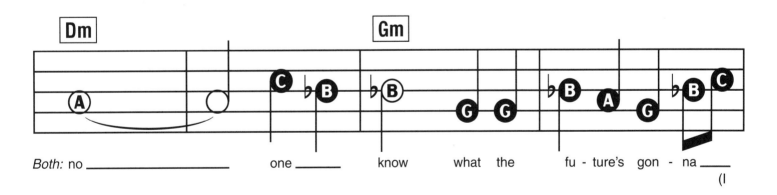

Both: no _____ one _____ know what the fu - ture's gon - na _____
(I

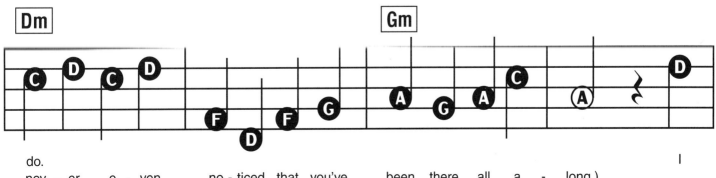

do.
nev - er e - ven no - ticed that you've been there all a - long.)
I

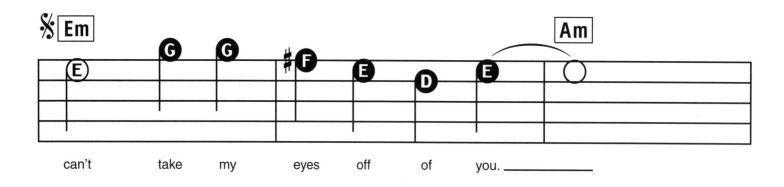

can't   take   my   eyes   off   of   you. _____

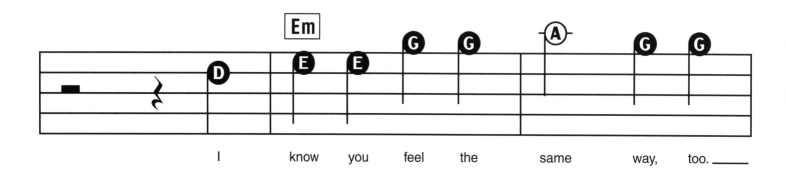

I   know   you   feel   the   same   way,   too. _____

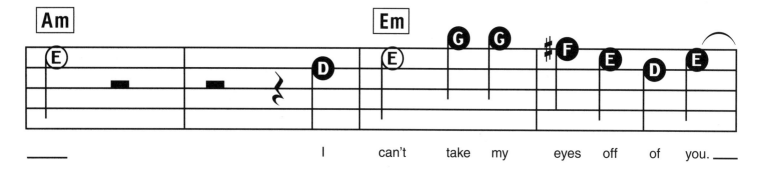

_____   I   can't   take   my   eyes   off   of   you. _____

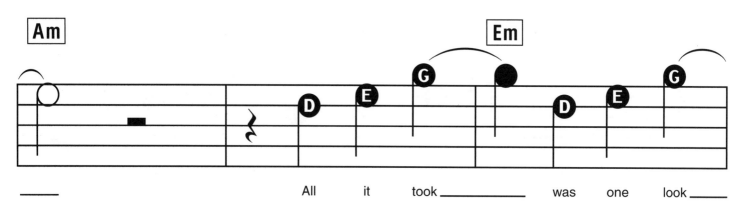

_____   All   it   took _____   was   one   look _____

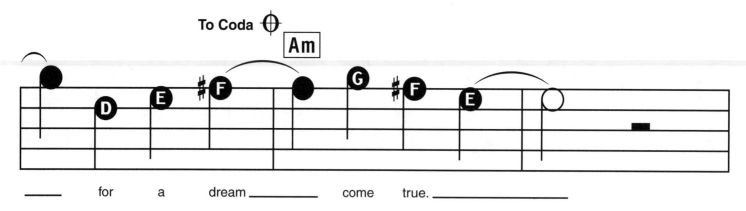

_____   for   a   dream _____   come   true. _____

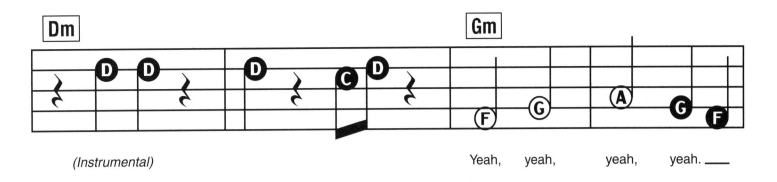

(Instrumental) Yeah, yeah, yeah, yeah. ___

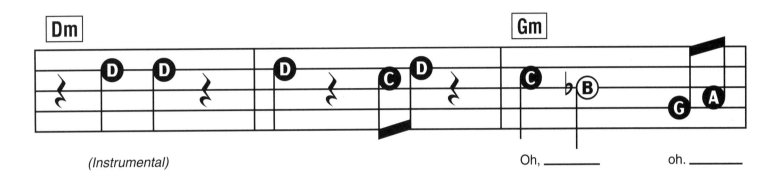

(Instrumental) Oh, ___ oh. ___

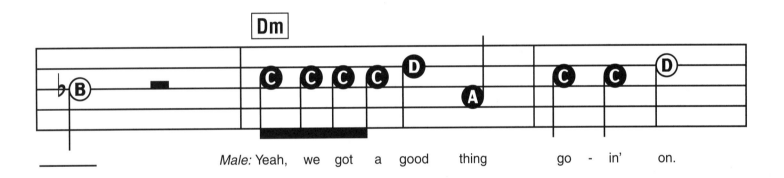

___ *Male:* Yeah, we got a good thing go - in' on.

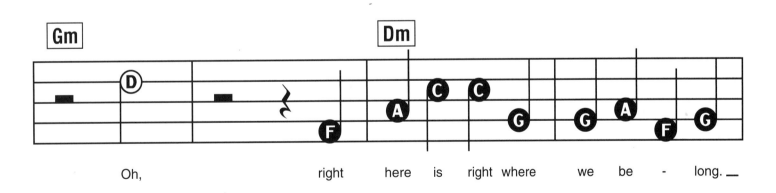

Oh, right here is right where we be - long. __

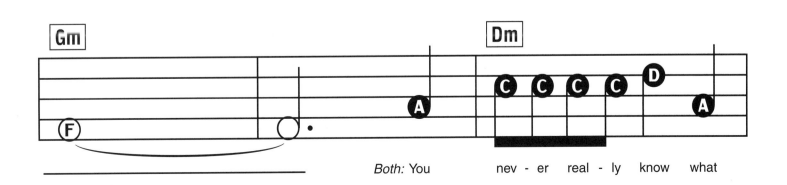

___ *Both:* You nev - er real - ly know what

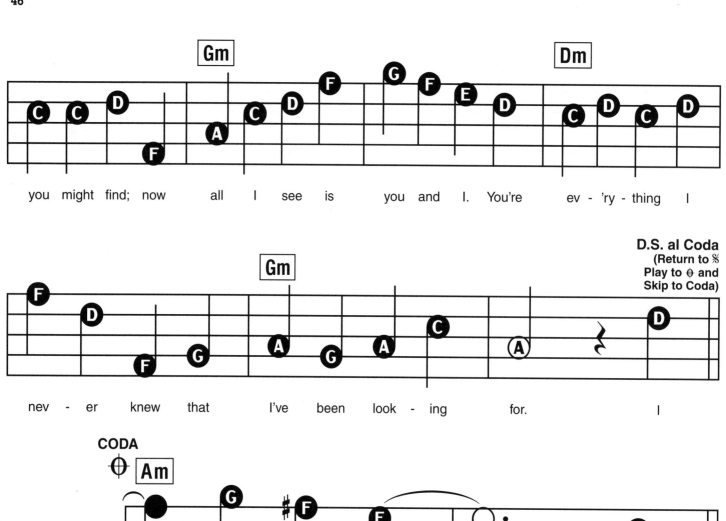

you might find; now all I see is you and I. You're ev - 'ry - thing I

D.S. al Coda
(Return to 𝄋
Play to ⊕ and
Skip to Coda)

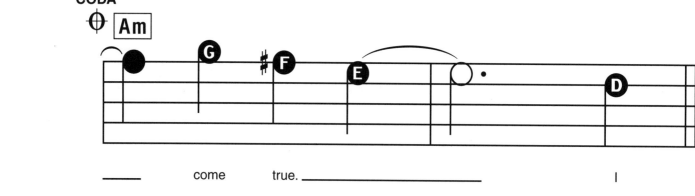

nev - er knew that I've been look - ing for. I

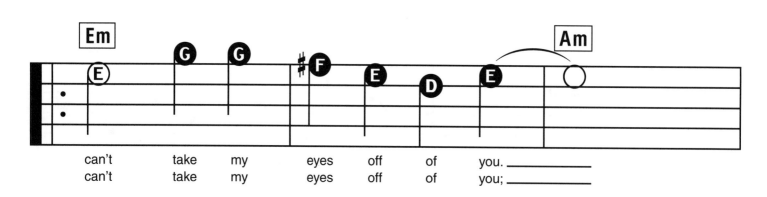

come true. I

can't take my eyes off of you. _____
can't take my eyes off of you; _____

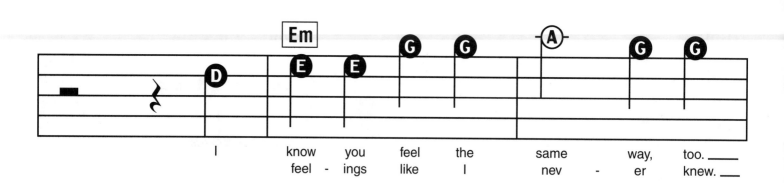

I know you feel the same way, too. ____
feel - ings like I nev - er knew. ___

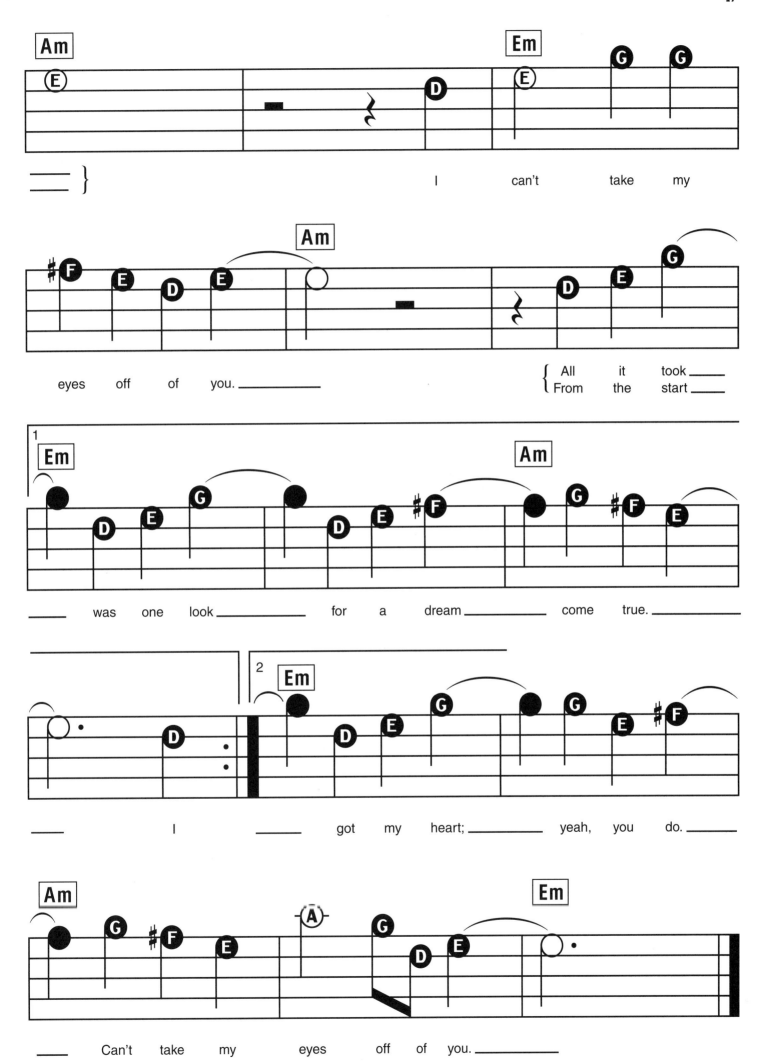